SUNDERLAND F.C.

– THE 25 YEAR RECORD

1971-72 to 1995-96 Seasons

SEASON BY SEASON WRITE-UPS
David Powter

EDITOR
Michael Robinson

CONTENTS

British Library Cataloguing in Publication Data
A catalogue record for this book is available from the British Library
ISBN 0-947808-88-4

Copyright © 1996; SOCCER BOOK PUBLISHING LTD. (01472-696226)
72, St. Peters' Avenue, Cleethorpes, N.E. Lincolnshire, DN35 8HU, England

Printed by Redwood Books, Kennet House, Kennet Way, Trowbridge, Wilts.

SUNDERLAND
– Seasons 1971-72 to 1995-96

The past 25 seasons have contained some swaying fortunes for Sunderland AFC. Having previously only spent seven years outside the top-flight, the last quarter of a century brought only seven top-flight seasons, in three different spells. While there was also the desolation of relegation to the Third Division for the first time, there were three Divisional titles and three visits to Wembley – not least the magnificent victory over Leeds United in 1973; when Bob Stokoe's side became the first from the Second Division for 42 years to hold aloft the F.A. Cup.

With the club deservedly securing the First Division Championship in 1995-96, Wearsiders have much to anticipate. Not only will they taste Premiership football for the first time, they also have the prospect of a superb new stadium on the horizon.

There was a lot less optimism twenty five seasons ago, in 1971-72, when the club started the second term of their second spell in Division Two. It was also Alan Brown's second spell as the club's manager – he had been at the helm both times they had been relegated and, peculiarly, had switched to Sheffield Wednesday in between, after leading the Wearsiders back up in 1963-64.

Sunderland were always among the promotion pack in 1971-72; but lacked a little consistency and finished fifth (six points adrift) after winning only four of their last 12 fixtures. Dave Watson and Denis Tueart were joint top scorers on the 13 goal mark.

They squandered a good start to 1972-73 and had been sucked into relegation trouble when Brown was sacked in the November. The board acted quickly to bring Blackpool boss Bob Stokoe to Roker Park. The new manager immediately got to grips with his task and his side only lost five times after Christmas to cut through the field and finish sixth. However, the club's League games formed only a sub-plot as the main focus was on their magnificent F.A. Cup run.

Replays were required at every stage up until the quarter-final. Third Division Notts County were finally defeated at Roker Park; resilient Reading (of the

Fourth Division) took Stokoe's side back to Elm Park before crumbling 3-1; while top-flight Manchester City were beaten in fine style by the same scoreline at Roker Park, following a 2-2 draw at Maine Road.

Second half goals by Watson and Ron Guthrie killed off fellow Division Two side Luton Town (at Roker Park) and ensured Sunderland reached the semi-final stage for the first time in 17 years. Their opponents at Hillsborough were Arsenal who, still holding hopes of collecting a second double, were clear favourites. However, it was to be the underdogs' day as Arsenal were outplayed. Goals by Vic Halom and Billy Hughes spiked the Londoners' guns and the Wearsiders were on the way to Wembley despite a reply by Charlie George.

Sunderland's first F.A. Cup final for 36 years was to be against Leeds United, whose 12 man squad contained 11 full internationals. Don Revie's side were hot favourites; but the Wearsiders harassed them out of their stride early on with their determined tackling. Then, following a 31st minute corner, the ball fell kindly off Halom's knee for Ian Porterfield to volley the Second Division side into the lead.

The atmosphere grew more and more electric in the second half as Leeds pushed their full-backs up and applied pressure from every angle. However, with keeper Jim Montgomery making a magnificent double save, Sunderland gritted their teeth and held on. There was an explosion of joy at the final whistle and few spectators or TV viewers will forget the image of Stokoe racing across the hallowed turf to hug his heroic keeper at the final whistle. Stokoe's Cup winning side was Montgomery, Dick Malone, Guthrie, Watson, Richie Pitt, Bobby Kerr (the skipper), Mick Horswill, Poterfield, Hughes, Halom and Tueart.

The F.A. Cup winners were naturally favourites to win promotion in 1973-74, but were soon brought back to earth when they failed to win any of their three opening home games. Sunderland lodged in mid table for most of the season, before winning 11 of their last 16 fixtures to finish sixth – a misleading two points short of the promotion line. Halom top scored (with 18), while Tueart and Horswill were the first members of the F.A. Cup winning side to leave Roker Park (for Manchester City, with Tony Towers moving in the opposite direction).

Although First Division Derby County had been defeated in the League Cup (before Liverpool knocked them out in the third round), there was no F.A. Cup glory in 1973-74, as they exited to Carlisle in a third round replay at Roker Park.

Sunderland enjoyed some success in the Cup Winners' Cup, beating Vasas Budapest 2-0 in Hungary and following up with a 1-0 win at Roker Park. They then defeated Sporting Lisbon 2-1 in the second round first leg, before exiting (2-0) in front of 50,000 in Lisbon.

Stokoe recruited two ex-Newcastle players, Bobby Moncur and Bryan Robson (from West Ham), to bolster the squad for 1974-75. His settled side performed consistently and were wedged in second place (behind Manchester United) for much of the season. They hit a sticky patch in February and March, winning only won one match in seven and letting Aston Villa go past them. Sunderland eventually were pushed into fourth place – just two points short of promotion. Robson was the leading marksman with 19.

The long overdue promotion was gained in 1975-76 when Stokoe's side finished three points in front of both Bristol City and WBA, to clinch the Second Division Championship. They first topped the table during a golden spell of 13 wins from 16 matches up until the end of November. They wobbled a little after Christmas, when they were perhaps distracted slightly by another F.A. Cup run, but finished strongly (winning six of their last eight) to take the Crown. It had been the side's solid defence (which conceded only 36 goals) and their unbeaten home record (won 19 and drew 2) that had seen them through.

Oldham, Hull City and top-flight Stoke (in a replay) were all defeated at Roker Park in the F.A. Cup, before Sunderland lost to giant killers Crystal Palace (of the Third Division) who were the only visiting side to win on Wearside that season.

The key members of Stokoe's squad in that excellent 1975-76 campaign were Montgomery, Malone, Joe Bolton, Jack Ashurst, Jeff Clarke, Moncur, Towers, Kerr, Porterfield, Halom, Robson (who top scored with 13) and Mel Holden (who scored 12). In addition, Roy Greenwood and Ray Train made important contributions after arriving in the new year.

There was no happy return to the First Division as the club were relegated after one term. It all went wrong from the start when, with goals hard to come by, there were no victories in the first nine games. Then, surprisingly, Bob Stokoe resigned - a decision he later regretted.

The first win was at Coventry in the 11th game, under the stewardship of caretaker Ian MacFarland. He later became assistant to the new manager Jimmy Adamson, who took over at the end of November. Ten games without a goal, which embraced nine successive defeats, appeared to have left the club doomed in bottom place; but Adamson reshuffled his resources and a run of just two defeats from 18 games pulled them out of the relegation zone with one match of the 1976-77 campaign remaining.

That final game at Everton was lost 2-0; but Sunderland would still have been safe if the game on the same night between the two other relegation threatened clubs, Coventry and Bristol City, did not end in a draw. The match at Highfield Road had kicked off late and, with the score standing at 2-2, the final score from Goodison Park was flashed up on the electronic scoreboard. Not surprisingly, both teams just 'played out' the remaining time and Sunderland were left marooned in 20th place – one point adrift of Coventry and Bristol City.

A notable departure from Roker Park during the 1976-77 campaign was Jim Montgomery, who joined Birmingham City, after making a club record 537 League appearances.

A poor start, of just one win from the first ten games, reduced Sunderland's chances of an instant return to the First Division. Nevertheless a turnaround in form propelled them into the promotion pack in November. However, they faded and it was only an end of season surge that pushed them back to finish sixth. Gary Rowell was the main marksman in 1977-78, with 18.

Sunderland looked more business-like in the early part of the following season and were lying in eighth place when Adamson was lured away to manage Leeds United at the end of October. Former player Billy Elliott took the reins on a caretaker basis and there was no loss in form.

Elliott's side moved into the top three during March; but, despite winning 13 of their last 18 fixtures, they just missed out on promotion by one point and one place as they finished fourth. A 2-1 home defeat by Cardiff in the penultimate match was a major blow, although the Wearsiders stayed in third spot after winning their last match at Wrexham. However, six days later, Crystal Palace won a rearranged fixture to leap to promotion and push the Rokerites into fourth place.

Rowell top scored with 21 goals in 1978-79, the season that Bobby Kerr – the final survivor from the F.A. Cup winning side – made his 368th and last League appearance for the club.

It was coach Ken Knighton, rather than Elliott, who was appointed manager for the following campaign, while a significant re-addition to playing resources was Bryan Robson (who had returned to West Ham three years before). Knighton's side started confidently and were always among the promotion pack. They secured promotion in second place (one point behind Leicester) with a 14 game unbeaten run.

Robson top scored (with 20), while Stan Cummins netted 12 times after his November arrival from Middlesbrough. The other key members of Knighton's 1979-80 squad were goalkeeper Chris Turner, Steve Whitworth, Shaun Elliott, Rob Hindmarch, Kevin Arnott, Alan Brown, Jeff Clarke and the long serving Joe Bolton.

Sunderland had also enjoyed a little success in the League Cup in 1979-80, knocking out Newcastle and First Division Manchester City, before being defeated by West Ham in a fourth round replay.

Knighton's side started well in 1980-81, beating Everton (at home) and Manchester City 4-0 at Maine Road. However, they could not sustain that form and soon found themselves at the wrong end of the table. Four victories from the last nine games just saved them and they finished 17th, two points clear of danger. However, there was no reprieve for Knighton who was replaced for the 1981-82 campaign by Alan Durban.

The Wearsiders made a dire start, winning only once in the first third of the season when they went eight games without finding the net. There was gradual improvement, but Sunderland were still deep in relegation trouble (one off the bottom) when they awoke from their slumbers, in April, and won six of the last ten matches (including the crucial last match at home to Manchester City) to avoid the drop by two points in 19th place.

Durban's side failed to score in 20 League matches in 1981-82 and netted just 38 goals, nine of which were hit by Rowell – the top scorer.

After collecting seven points from their opening three fixtures of 1982-83, Sunderland were derailed by four successive defeats including an 8-0 hammering at Watford. Having won just four games, they were deep in relegation trouble at the halfway stage; but lost only six more times to finish 16th.

Four defeats in the first six games alerted Rokerites that 1983-84 would be another season of struggle. There was some improvement, although it was not enough to save Durban from the sack in the March. He was replaced by former Sunderland player Len Ashurst. Four wins from the last seven matches were enough to secure the Wearsiders 13th place. They had scored on average exactly a goal a game, with Colin West heading the scorers' list on the nine goal mark.

The following season promised so much, but sadly ended in disaster. A burst of three wins in four games took Ashurst's side up to seventh place in early November; but thereafter they plummeted towards the Second Division. Their best form was reserved for Milk Cup ties – Crystal Palace, Nottingham Forest, Spurs (in a White Hart Lane replay) and Watford were knocked out to set up a two legged semi-final with Chelsea. A brace by West gave the Wearsiders a two goal cushion for the trip to Stamford Bridge, where another by West and two by Clive Walker gave them a 3-2 win and killed off the Blues to secure a Wembley place.

Their opponents in the Milk Cup final were fellow relegation strugglers Norwich City. Only one second half effort separated the sides at the end and, although the goal was credited to a Sunderland player, it was the Canaries who collected the trophy. Asa Hartford's winning shot deflected into the net off Gordon Chisholm.

Ironically both Milk Cup finalists were relegated in 1984-85. Sunderland only won three times in the second half of the season, netted only 40 times all term and finished 21st, ten points adrift of safety. Ashurst was sacked and replaced by long-time Southampton boss Lawrie McMenemy during the summer of 1985.

McMenemy's side made an appalling start, losing the first five, and didn't win until the eighth game (at Shrewsbury). They gradually improved, before fading back into relegation trouble in the new year. They just survived by winning three of their last four games to finish 1985-86 in 18th place, four points clear of relegation.

After a mixed start, Sunderland looked on course to push for promotion in

1986-87 when they moved into fifth spot at the end of October. However, a continued lack of fire-power hindered them and they drifted towards the wrong end of the table. McMenemy departed in April during a spell of six defeats in seven and Bob Stokoe was handed the reins again on a caretaker basis.

A 3-2 home defeat on the last day of the season consigned the Wearsiders to 20th place and forced them to participate in the play-offs. Despite another 3-2 defeat at Gillingham in the semi-final first leg, Sunderland fancied their chances of progressing to the final. However, it was not to be as the Gills went through on away goals. The score after 90 minutes at Roker Park was 3-2 to the home side, before both sides netted again in extra-time. For the first time in their history, Sunderland were a Third Division club.

The man handed the task of getting the club back on an even keel was Denis Smith. He rose to the challenge and led the Wearsiders to the Third Division title and promotion at the first attempt.

Five successive victories in October underlined the club's challenge and took them to the top of the table. A 15 match unbeaten run that spanned November through to the middle of February kept them in the lead. They wobbled and dropped behind Notts County for the whole of March; but found a second wind to win seven of the last eight matches and take the title by a margin of nine points.

Sunderland collected a club record 93 points and scored 92 goals in 1987-88. The main marksman was Marco Gabbiadini, who had followed Smith from York, with 21. The other regular members of Smith's squad were goalkeeper Iain Hesford, John Kay, Reuben Agboola, Gary Bennett, Eric Gates (who netted 19), John MacPhail (who netted 16 including 10 from the spot), Gordon Armstrong, Paul Lemon, Gary Owers, Stephen Doyle and Frankie Gray (whose 34 appearances included 22 as a sub).

The Wearsiders made a sticky start to their return to the second-flight and were without a win after the first six games of 1988-89. However, four wins from six games took them into mid-table and they finished a season of consolidation in 11th place. Gabbiadini again top scored, with 18.

Marco Gabbiadini was also the top scorer (on 21) the following season as Sunderland regained their First Division status. Smith's side were always among the leading pack, but couldn't force their way through to take an automatic promotion place in 1989-90. Instead they finished sixth to earn a stab at the play-offs.

Their prospects dimmed after being held to a goalless draw, at home, by Newcastle in the first leg of the semi-final. However, goals by Gates and Gabbiadini gave Sunderland a superb 2-0 win in front of over 32,000 at St James' Park. That earned the Wearsiders a trip to Wembley and a final with Swindon Town. The Wiltshire side deservedly won the day with a single first half goal (deflected off Bennett) and Sunderland appeared consigned to another season of Second Division football.

However, within ten days, Swindon were rocked as the Football League sanctioned them for 'financial irregularities' and relegated them. Shortly afterwards it was confirmed that Sunderland would fill the vacant top-flight place. Although its club was entering the First Division via the cat-flap of the back-door, Wearside was overjoyed.

That joy evaporated as Sunderland slid straight back to the second-flight, winning only eight games during 1990-91. They only netted 38 goals (nine by Gabbiadini) in the same number of games to finish 19th, one place off the bottom. They collected three points fewer than 'safe' Luton Town, and might have saved themselves on the final day, but lost 3-2 away at Manchester City.

Marco Gabbiadini departed to Crystal Palace for a club record £1.5 million in September after netting 74 goals in 157 League games and having topped the Roker scorers' list for four successive seasons.

Sunderland made a mediocre start to 1991-92 and were struggling in 17th place when Smith and his coach Viv Busby were sacked at the end of December. Malcolm Crosby, the youth team manager, was handed the reins on a temporary basis. Despite a few traumas (not least 7 defeats in 8 games), Crosby steered the club to safety (by five points) in 18th place.

Meanwhile, for the second time in their history, Sunderland reached the F.A. Cup final as a Second Division side. Fellow second-flight sides Port Vale and Oxford were defeated, before Crosby's side met West Ham in the fifth round. The First Division side were happy with a draw at Roker Park, but it was Sunderland who won the replay.

Another top-flight London side, Chelsea, were the quarter-final opponents.

After a 1-1 draw at Stamford Bridge, it was Sunderland who again triumphed in a replay to set up a semi-final meeting with Norwich at Hillsborough. The Norfolk side were favourites to reach their first F.A. Cup final; but their dream was pierced by a single first half effort by John Byrne.

Sunderland were again the underdogs at Wembley as they faced Graeme Souness's Liverpool. Although they gave a good account of themselves Crosby's team could not repeat the feat of Stokoe's 1973 side and were beaten 2-0. The losing finalists in 1992 were goalkeeper Tony Norman, Owers, Kevin Ball, Bennett, Anton Rogan, David Rush, Paul Bracewell, Peter Davenport, Armstrong, Byrne and Brian Atkinson. Paul Hardyman and Warren Hawke came on as substitutes.

Crosby had been appointed manager on a permanent basis shortly before the final. However, he was never to see out a full season in the hot-seat. His side struggled badly and had won only eight of the first 25 games when he was sacked on 1st February 1993. Former England defender Terry Butcher (who had joined the club in the close season) was quickly appointed the new player-manager.

Despite losing seven of their last ten matches, Butcher's side just avoided relegation in 1992-93, by one point in 21st place. Sunderland only survived on the last day despite being beaten at Notts County, because Brentford lost rather than drew at Bristol City.

The 1993-94 campaign started sourly with a 5-0 defeat at Derby. The board's patience with Butcher ran out towards the end of November with the club in 20th place, having lost five successive games. Mick Buxton was appointed as the new manager and gradually his side hauled themselves out of trouble. They finished in 12th place with Phil Gray top scoring on the 14 goal mark. Earlier in the term, they experienced some glory in the Coca-Cola Cup by defeating Premiership Leeds United 2-1 twice in the second round (before exiting to Aston Villa at the next stage).

For the fourth successive campaign, Sunderland changed managers in mid-term in 1994-95. Buxton's side had climbed as high as eighth in the October, before losing their way and spinning into relegation trouble. Buxton was replaced by Peter Reid at the end of March and the one-time Manchester City boss led the Wearsiders to safety. They lost just once during the last seven games and finished 20th, six points above the relegation line.

Sunderland returned to the top-flight with a beautifully timed challenge for the 1995-96 First Division Championship. Reid's side performed consistently all term and moved into the top four during December. By the end of January they were in third place and then hit the front in March. They stayed on to take the title with 83 points, four more than Derby County. Craig Russell was the top scorer with 13 out of a total of 59 goals. However, Sunderland's best work was carried out at the other end, where their two keepers, Alec Chamberlain and on-loan Shay Given, conceded only 33 goals and collected a phenomenal 26 clean sheets.

The other key members of Reid's squad in 1995-96 were Ball (the captain), Bracewell, Dariusz Kubicki, Richard Ord, Andy Melville, Martin Scott, Lee Howey, Steve Agnew, Phil Gray and the exciting Michael Gray.

Sunderland supporters have much to look forward to – both on and off the field. Their club is one of the top twenty in the country and, during 1997, they will have an excellent new stadium, at nearby Monkwearmouth.

Views of Roker Park – Sunderland FC's home since 1898. Sunderland plan to move to a new 40,000 seater at Monkwearmouth in 1997.

1971-72

1	Aug	14	(h)	Birmingham C	D	1-1	Watson	9,749
2		21	(a)	Watford	D	1-1	Porterfield	11,283
3		28	(h)	Orient	W	2-0	Tueart, Kerr	14,544
4	Sep	1	(h)	Carlisle U	L	0-3		20,998
5		4	(a)	Millwall	D	1-1	Watson	12,446
6		11	(h)	Swindon T	W	1-0	Chambers	12,811
7		18	(a)	Sheffield W	L	0-3		13,710
8		25	(h)	Preston NE	W	4-3	Pitt, Tueart 2, Hamilton	13,102
9		29	(h)	Middlesbrough	W	4-1	Kerr, Watson, Tueart, Hughes	28,129
10	Oct	2	(a)	Burnley	W	1-0	Watson	16,432
11		9	(h)	Norwich C	D	1-1	Tueart	24,951
12		16	(a)	Birmingham C	D	1-1	Kerr	27,341
13		19	(a)	Charlton A	D	2-2	Hughes, Warman (og)	8,133
14		23	(a)	Oxford U	L	0-2		10,735
15		30	(h)	Luton T	D	2-2	Watson, McGiven	17,979
16	Nov	6	(a)	Portsmouth	D	2-2	Watson, Tueart	14,387
17		13	(h)	Blackpool	D	0-0		17,240
18		20	(a)	Cardiff C	W	2-1	Hughes, Kerr	12,735
19		27	(h)	Bristol C	D	1-1	Pitt	15,655
20	Dec	4	(a)	Queen's Park R	L	1-2	Kerr	13,576
21		11	(h)	Fulham	W	2-1	Hughes, Tueart	11,833
22		18	(h)	Millwall	D	3-3	Pitt, Hughes, Kerr	16,484
23		27	(a)	Hull C	W	3-2	Pitt, Tueart, Hughes	26,091
24	Jan	1	(h)	Sheffield W	W	2-0	Kerr, Tueart	23,228
25		8	(a)	Orient	L	0-5		6,966
26		22	(a)	Middlesbrough	L	0-2		34,856
27		29	(h)	Charlton A	W	3-0	Chambers 2, Hughes	12,877
28	Feb	12	(h)	Oxford U	W	3-0	Tueart 2, Porterfield	15,368
29		19	(a)	Luton T	W	2-1	Pitt, Tueart	10,994
30	Mar	1	(h)	Portsmouth	W	3-2	Lathan 3	8,273
31		4	(a)	Blackpool	D	1-1	Watson	10,989
32		11	(a)	Norwich C	D	1-1	Harvey	22,143
33		25	(a)	Swindon T	D	1-1	Lathan	12,102
34	Apr	1	(h)	Hull C	L	0-1		17,621
35		3	(h)	Burnley	W	4-3	Watson 2, Coleman, Hughes	14,034
36		4	(a)	Preston NE	W	3-1	Watson, Porterfield, Tueart	13,450
37		8	(h)	Cardiff C	D	1-1	Watson	15,224
38		15	(a)	Bristol C	L	1-3	Kerr	12,178
39		17	(h)	Watford	W	5-0	Watson 2, McGiven, Porterfield, Pitt	8,981
40		22	(h)	Queen's Park R	L	0-1		13,751
41		25	(a)	Carlisle U	W	2-1	Porterfield, Kerr	10,326
42		29	(a)	Fulham	D	0-0		12,360

FINAL LEAGUE POSITION: 5th in Division Two

Appearances

Sub. Appearances

Goals

Montgomery	Malone	Park	Harvey	Pitt	Porterfield	McGiven	Kerr	Watson	Harris	Hughes	Tueart	Irwin	Symm	Chambers	Coleman	McIver	Lowrey	Lathan	Hamilton	Taylor	Forster	Horswill	Bolton	No.
1	2	3*	4	5	6	7	8	9	10	11	12													1
1	2		6	5	8	4	7	9	10*	11	12	3												2
1	2	6*	5	10	4	7	9			11	8	3	12						-					3
1	2		4	5	6	7	10	9		11	8	3												4
1	2		4	5	10		8	9		12	11	3	6	7*										5
1	2		4	5	10		7	9		12	11	6*		8	3									6
1	2		4	5	6		8	9			11*			7	3		10	12						7
1	2		4	5	6		8	9			11			7*	3		10		12					8
1	2		4	5	6	7	8	9		12	11				3				10*					9
1	2		4	5	6	7	8	9		12	11				3				10*					10
1	2		4	5	6	7*	8	9		12	11			10	3									11
1	2		4	5	6	7	8	9			11			12	3				10*					12
1	2		4	5	6		8	9		7	11			10	3*				12					13
1	2		3	5	6	7	8	9		12	11				3				10*					14
1	2		4	5	6*	7	8	9		10	11				3				12					15
1	2		4	5	6		8	9		10	11			7	3									16
1	2		4	5	6		8	9		10	11*			3	3				12					17
1	2		4	5	6		8	9*		11	10			7	3				12					18
1	2		5	6		4	8	9		10	11			7	3									19
1	2		4	5*		7	8	9		10	11			6	3				12					20
	2		5		10	4*	8	9		7	11			6	3				12	1				21
	2		4	5	10*		8	9		7	11			6	3				12	1				22
	2		4	5	6		8	9		10	11			7	3					1				23
	2		4	5	6		8	9		10	11			7	3					1				24
	2		4	5	6		8	9		10	11			7*	3					1				25
1	2		4	5	10		8	9		7	11			6	3									26
1	2		4	5	6		8	9		10	11			7	3									27
1	2		4	5	8	6		9		10*	11			7	3				12					28
	2		4	5	7	6	8	9			11				3			10		1				29
	2		4	5	6	7	8	9			11				3			10		1				30
	2		12	5	6	7	8*	9			11			4	3			10		1				31
1	2		3	5	6	7	8	9			11			4	3			10						32
1	2			5	6	7	8	9			11			4	3			10						33
1	2			5	6	7	8	9		12	11*			4	3			10						34
1	2			5	6	7	8	9		12	11			4	3			10*						35
	2			5	6	7	8	9		10	11				3					1	4			36
	2			5	6	7	8	9		10*	11*				3				12	1	4			37
	2			5	6	7	8	9		12	11				3			10		1	4			38
1	2			5	12	7	8	9			11			6*				10			4	3		39
1				5	6	7	8	9		12	11				2			10*			4	3		40
1	2			5	6	7	8	9			11							10			4	3		41
1	2			5	6*	7	8	9		12	11							10			4	3		42
31	41	1	31	41	36	31	41	42	2	21	40	4	2	25	32	1	2	12	4	11	7	4		
			1		1	1				11	2		1	1				7		3	1			
			1	6	5	2	9	13		8	13			3	1			4	1					

1972-73

1	Aug	12	(a)	Middlesbrough	L	1-2	Lathan	28,853
2		19	(h)	Orient	W	1-0	Tueart	12,658
3		26	(a)	Brighton & HA	D	2-2	Lathan 2	15,906
4		28	(a)	Blackpool	D	0-0		14,797
5	Sep	2	(h)	Swindon T	W	3-2	Tueart, Lathan, Kerr	11,674
6		9	(a)	Millwall	W	1-0	Tueart	9,817
7		16	(h)	Sheffield W	D	1-1	Tueart (pen)	16,960
8		23	(a)	Huddersfield T	D	1-1	Porterfield	10,145
9		26	(a)	Aston Villa	L	0-2		29,895
10		30	(h)	Nottingham F	W	4-1	Lathan 2, Porterfield, Hughes W	14,155
11	Oct	7	(a)	Oxford U	L	1-5	Kerr	8,881
12		14	(h)	Luton T	L	0-2		13,394
13		21	(a)	Queen's Park R	L	2-3	Tueart, Hamilton	17,356
14		28	(h)	Fulham	D	0-0		11,618
15	Nov	4	(h)	Aston Villa	D	2-2	Hughes W, Kerr	18,717
16		11	(a)	Carlisle U	L	3-4	Porterfield 2, Lathan	8,884
17		18	(h)	Hull C	D	1-1	Coleman	11,141
18		25	(a)	Bristol C	L	0-1		10,666
19	Dec	2	(h)	Burnley	L	0-1		16,812
20		9	(a)	Portsmouth	W	3-2	Watson, Hughes W, Kerr	5,783
21		16	(h)	Preston NE	D	0-0		11,529
22	Jan	6	(h)	Brighton & HA	W	4-0	Hughes W 2, Tueart, Bolton	12,573
23		20	(a)	Swindon T	D	1-1	Porterfield	7,010
24		27	(h)	Millwall	W	2-0	Tueart, Kerr	22,781
25	Feb	10	(a)	Sheffield W	L	0-1		16,949
26		17	(h)	Middlesbrough	W	4-0	Horswill, Halom, Hughes W, Tueart	25,840
27	Mar	3	(h)	Oxford U	W	1-0	Watson	39,222
28		10	(a)	Luton T	L	0-1		12,458
29		19	(a)	Preston NE	W	3-1	Hughes W 2, Halom	7,636
30		24	(a)	Fulham	W	2-1	Tueart (pen), Halom	9,645
31		27	(h)	Carlisle U	W	2-1	Hughes W, Tueart (pen)	39,930
32		31	(h)	Bristol C	D	2-2	Merrick (og), Watson	33,255
33	Apr	10	(h)	Huddersfield T	W	3-0	Hughes W 3	32,251
34		14	(h)	Portsmouth	W	2-0	Kerr, Tueart (pen)	31,430
35		16	(a)	Burnley	L	0-2		22,896
36		21	(a)	Hull C	W	2-0	Halom, Hughes W	12,637
37		23	(h)	Cardiff C	W	2-1	Tueart (pen), Hughes W	27,551
38		24	(a)	Nottingham F	L	0-1		10,306
39		28	(h)	Blackpool	W	1-0	Hughes W	26,921
40		30	(a)	Orient	D	1-1	Young	9,157
41	May	7	(a)	Cardiff C	D	1-1	Halom	26,008
42		9	(h)	Queen's Park R	L	0-3		43,265

FINAL LEAGUE POSITION: 6th in Division Two

Appearances

Sub. Appearances

Goals

16

Montgomery	Malone	Bolton	Horswill	Pitt	Porterfield	McGivern	Kerr	Hamilton	Lathan	Tueart	Tones	Watson	Coleman	Hughes W	Ashurst	Chambers	Young	Guthrie	Hughes J	Halom	Ellison	Swinburne	
1	2	3	4	5	6	7	8	9*	10	11	12												1
1	2	3	4	5	6	7	8	12	10*	11		9											2
1	2		4	5	6	7	8	12	10*	11		9	3										3
1	2		4	5	6	7	8		10*	11		9	3	12									4
1	2		4	5	6	7	8		10	11		9	3										5
1	2		4		6	7	8		10*	11		9	3	12	5								6
1	2		4		6	7	8		10*	11		9	3	12	5								7
1	2		4		6	7	8		10*	11		9	3	12	5								8
1	2		4		6*		8	12	10	11		9	3	7	5								9
1	2		4		6		8		10	11		9	3	7	5								10
1	2		4		6		8	12	10	11		9	3	7*	5								11
1	2		4		6		8		10	11		9	3	7	5								12
1	2	3	4	5	6	7	8	9	10	11													13
1	2	3	4	5	6	7	8	12	10*	11		9											14
1	2		4	5	6		8			11		9	3	7		10							15
1	2		4		6		8	10*	12	11		5	3	9		7							16
1	2		4		6		8		10	11	12	5	3	9		7*							17
1	2		4		6		8		10	11		5	3	9		7							18
1	2		4		6		8		10*	11	12	5	3	9		7							19
1	2		4		6	10	8			11	12	5	3	9		7*							20
1	2		10		6	7*	8			11	4	5	3	9		12							21
1	2	3	4		10	12	7		9*	11		5		8			6						22
1	2		4		10	7*			12	11		9		8		6	5	3					23
1	2		4		10		8			11		5		7			6	3		9			24
1	2		4		10		8			11		5		7		12	6*	3		9			25
1	2		4	6	10		8			11		5		7				3		9			26
1	2		4*	6	10		7			11		5		8		12		3		9			27
1		12			10				11	8		5			4	7	6	3		9	2*		28
1	2		4	6	10		7			11		5		8*		12		3		9			29
1	2	3	4	6	10		7			11		5		8						9			30
1	2	3	4	6*	10		7			11		5		8		12				9			31
1	2		4	5	10		7			11		9		8			6	3					32
1	2		4*	6	10		7			11		5		8		12		3		9			33
1	2		4	6	10		7			11		5		8*		12		3		9			34
1	2	12	4	6	10		7			9		5		8*		11		3					35
1	2				10	12	7*			11				8	5	4	6	3		9			36
1	2	3			10*	12	7			11				8	5	4	6			9			37
1	2	12	4		8		7		9	11		5				10	6	3*					38
1	2		4	6	10		7			11*		5		8		12		3		9			39
	2		4	6	10		7					5		8		11		3		9	1		40
1	2	3	4	6	10		7			11		5		8*		12				9			41
1	2		4	6	10		7			11		5		8				3		9			42
41	41	9	39	21	40	14	41	4	20	40	2	37	17	29	11	11	11	15	1	15	2	1	
	3				3		5	2		4				4			6	3					
		1	1		5		6	1	7	12		3	1	15			1			5			

17

1973-74

#	Month	Date		Opponent	Res	Score	Scorers	Attendance
1	Aug	25	(h)	Orient	D	1-1	Hughes	28,211
2	Sep	1	(a)	Notts Co	W	4-1	Halom 2, Tueart, Hughes	15,335
3		8	(h)	Cardiff C	D	1-1	Guthrie	29,495
4		11	(a)	Portsmouth	D	1-1	Halom	18,989
5		15	(a)	Oxford U	W	1-0	Tueart	9,022
6		22	(h)	Luton T	L	0-1		27,582
7		29	(a)	West Brom A	D	1-1	Halom	17,027
8	Oct	6	(h)	Sheffield W	W	3-1	Hughes, Porterfield, Halom	28,955
9		13	(a)	Preston NE	·	L	0-1		21,747
10		20	(a)	Fulham	W	2-0	Horswill, Mullery (og)	14,971
11		27	(h)	Crystal Palace	D	0-0		31,935
12	Nov	3	(a)	Hull C	L	0-2		17,409
13		10	(h)	Swindon T	W	4-1	Tueart 3, Halom	24,636
14		13	(h)	Bolton W	W	3-0	Halom, Tueart (pen), Porterfield	26,454
15		17	(a)	Bristol C	L	0-2		14,965
16		24	(h)	Nottingham F	D	0-0		22,252
17	Dec	1	(a)	Blackpool	W	2-0	Belfitt, Halom	11,000
18		5	(a)	Bolton W	L	0-1		8,425
19		8	(h)	Aston Villa	W	2-0	Tueart, Halom	20,784
20		15	(a)	Millwall	L	1-2	Horswill	7,570
21		22	(h)	West Brom A	D	1-1	Tueart	18,389
22		26	(a)	Middlesbrough	L	1-2	Tueart (pen)	37,038
23		29	(a)	Cardiff C	L	1-4	Halom	14,799
24	Jan	1	(h)	Notts C	L	1-2	Halom	22,578
25		12	(h)	Oxford U	D	0-0		16,809
26		19	(a)	Orient	L	1-2	Belfitt	14,533
27	Feb	2	(h)	Millwall	W	4-0	Halom 2, Hughes 2	17,486
28		16	(h)	Preston NE	W	2-1	Belfitt, Halom	21,129
29		23	(a)	Sheffield W	W	1-0	Halom	17,816
30	Mar	2	(h)	Middlesbrough	L	0-2		41,658
31		5	(h)	Portsmouth	W	3-0	Tueart 2 (1 pen), Kerr	8,142
32		9	(a)	Crystal Palace	L	0-3		16,529
33		16	(h)	Fulham	W	1-0	Longhorn	20,730
34		23	(a)	Swindon T	W	2-0	Watson, Halom	6,178
35		30	(h)	Hull C	W	1-0	Hughes (pen)	21,418
36	Apr	6	(a)	Nottingham F	D	2-2	Hughes, Watson	18,044
37		12	(h)	Carlisle U	W	2-1	Halom, Hughes	34,179
38		13	(h)	Bristol C	L	1-2	Longhorn	28,884
39		16	(a)	Carlisle U	L	0-1		19,692
40		20	(a)	Aston Villa	W	2-1	McMahon (og), Watson	17,321
41		27	(h)	Blackpool	W	2-1	Towers, Kerr	22,331
42	May	1	(a)	Luton T	W	4-3	Hughes, Ashurst, Towers, Halom	20,285

FINAL LEAGUE POSITION: 6th in Division Two

Appearances

Sub. Appearances

Goals

Montgomery	Malone	Guthrie	McGiven	Watson	Young	Kerr	Hughes	Halom	Porterfield	Tueart	Bolton	Pitt	Horswill	Lathan	Ashurst	Belfitt	Mitchell	Hegan	Swinburne	Longhorn	Tower	Hamilton	
1	2	3	4*	5	6	7	8	9	10	11	12												1
1	2	3	4	5	6	7	8	9	10	11													2
1	2	3	4	5		7	8	9	10	11		6											3
1	2	3	4	5		7	8	9	10	11		6											4
1	2	3		5		7	8	9	10	11		6	4										5
1	2			5	12	7	8	9	10	11	3	6	4*										6
1	2	3		5	6	7	8	9	10	11			4										7
1	2	3		5	6	7	8	9	10	11*			4	12									8
1	2	3			6	7	8	9	10	11			4*	12	5								9
1	2	3*		5	6	7	8	9	10	11	12		4										10
1	2		.	5	6	7	8	9	10	11*	3		4		12								11
1	2	10	8	5	6						3		4	7		9	11						12
1	2			5		7		9	10	11	3		4		6	8							13
1	2			5		7		9	10	11	3		4		6	8							14
1	2			5		7	12	9	10	11	3		4		6*	8							15
1	2			5		7		9	10		3		4	11	6	8*	12						16
1	2			5		7	11	9	10		3		4		6	8							17
1	2			5		7	11	9	10	12	3		4*		6	8							18
1	2			5		7	8	9	10	11	3		4		6								19
1	2			5		7	11		10		3		4		6	9		8					20
1	2	3		5		7	8	9	10	11			4*		6	12							21
	2	3		5	6	7	8	9	10	11					4				1				22
1	2	3		5	6*	7	8	9	10	11			4			12							23
1	2			5	6	7		9	10*	11	3				12	8		4					24
1	2			5	6	7			10	11	3		12		4	9*		8					25
1	2			5	6	7			10	11	3		4*		8	9		12					26
1	2			5	12	7	8	9	10	11	3		4*			6							27
1	2			5		7	8	9	10	11	3		4			6							28
1	2			5		7	8	9	10	11	3		4			6							29
1	2			5		7	8	9	10	11	3		4*			6				12			30
1	2			5		7	8	9	10	11	3					6				4			31
1	2			5		7	11	9	10		3				8	6				4			32
1	2			5	12	7*	8	9	10		3					6				4	11		33
1	2			5		7	8	9	10		3					6				4	11		34
1	2			5		7	8	9	10		3					6				4	11		35
1	2			5		7	8	9	10*		3				12	6				4	11		36
1	2			5		7	8	9	10		3					6				4	11		37
1	2			5		7	8	9	10*		3				12	6				4	11		38
1	2	3		5		7	8	9	10		12				11*	6				4			39
1	2	3		5		7	8		10						6	9				4	11		40
1	2*	3		5		7	8	9	10						12	6				4	11		41
1	2	3		5		7	8	9							10	6				4	11		42
41	42	17	5	41	13	41	33	38	40	26	26	4	22	2	15	30	1	3	1	12	8	1	
					3	1					1	3	1	2	4	1	1	1		1			
		1	3		2	9	18	2		11			2		1	3				2	2		

1974-75

1	Aug	17	(a)	Millwall	W	4-1	Kerr, Towers, Halom, Hughes	10,573
2		24	(h)	Southampton	W	3-1	Watson, Robson, Hughes	34,021
3		31	(a)	West Brom A	L	0-1		12,732
4	Sep	7	(h)	Bristol R	W	5-1	Hughes 3 (1 pen), Aitken (og), Robson	24,010
5		14	(a)	York C	W	1-0	Halom	14,964
6		21	(h)	Bolton W	D	0-0		28,453
7		24	(h)	Norwich C	D	0-0		27,737
8		28	(a)	Nottingham F	D	1-1	Hughes (pen)	14,885
9	Oct	2	(a)	Sheffield W	W	2-0	Kerr, Hughes	11,490
10		5	(h)	Oxford U	W	2-0	Robson 2	27,594
11		12	(a)	Bristol C	D	1-1	Halom	13,084
12		15	(h)	Sheffield W	W	3-0	Hughes, Kerr, Watson	28,155
13		19	(h)	Aston Villa	D	0-0		33,232
14		26	(a)	Hull C	L	1-3	Robson	15,010
15	Nov	2	(a)	Cardiff C	L	0-2		9,883
16		9	(h)	Blackpool	W	1-0	Robson	24,939
17		16	(a)	Fulham	W	3-1	Moore (og), Robson 2	14,193
18		23	(h)	Notts Co	W	3-0	Porterfield, Robson 2	25,677
19		30	(a)	Manchester U	L	2-3	Hughes 2	60,585
20	Dec	7	(h)	Portsmouth	W	4-1	Halom, Hughes (pen), Malone, Robson	25,926
21		14	(h)	Millwall	W	2-0	Robson, Kerr	26,235
22		21	(a)	Oldham A	D	0-0		14,681
23		26	(h)	York C	W	2-0	Kerr 2	33,367
24		28	(a)	Orient	D	1-1	Hughes	10,029
25	Jan	11	(a)	Portsmouth	L	2-4	Robson, Halom	14,133
26		14	(a)	Southampton	D	1-1	Hughes	16,738
27		18	(h)	Manchester U	D	0-0		45,976
28	Feb	1	(a)	Blackpool	L	2-3	Halom, Kerr	16,151
29		8	(h)	Cardiff C	W	3-1	Towers (pen), Morgan (og), Robson	29,315
30		15	(a)	Notts Co	D	0-0		15,855
31		22	(h)	Fulham	L	1-2	Towers (pen)	33,418
32	Mar	1	(h)	West Brom A	W	3-0	Halom, Robson 2	28,867
33		8	(a)	Norwich C	D	0-0		29,285
34		15	(h)	Nottingham F	D	0-0		30,812
35		22	(a)	Bristol R	L	1-2	Robson	13,270
36		25	(h)	Oldham A	D	2-2	Robson, Watson	27,460
37		28	(h)	Orient	W	3-0	Watson, Hughes, Bolton	30,908
38		31	(a)	Bolton W	W	2-0	Hughes, Towers	18,220
39	Apr	5	(h)	Hull C	W	1-0	Halom	29,838
40		12	(a)	Oxford U	L	0-1		13,004
41		19	(h)	Bristol C	W	3-0	Bolton, Robson, Belfitt	30,530
42		26	(a)	Aston Villa	L	0-2		57,266

FINAL LEAGUE POSITION: 4th in Division Two

Appearances

Sub. Appearances

Goals

Montgomery	Malone	Guthrie	Longhorn	Watson	Moncur	Kerr	Hughes	Halom	Robson	Towers	Belfitt	Finney	Bolton	Ashurst	Porterfield	Swinburne	#
1	2	3	4	5	6	7	8	9	10	11							1
1	2	3	4	5	6	7	8	9*	10	11	12						2
1	2	3	4	5	6	7	8	9	10	11							3
1	2	3	4	5	6	7	8	9	10	11							4
1	2	3	4	5	6	7	8	9	10	11							5
1	2	3	4	5	6	7	8		10	11	9*	12					6
1	2				4	7	8		10	11	9		3	5	6		7
1	2			5	4	7	8		10	11	9		3		6		8
1	2			5	4	7	8	9	10	11			3		6		9
1	2			5	4	7	8		10	11	9*	12	3		6		10
1	2			5	4	7	8	9	10	11			3		6		11
1	2	3		5	4	7	8	9	10	11					6		12
1	2	3		5	4	7	8	9	10	11					6		13
1	2	3*		5	4	7	8	9	10	11		12			6		14
1	2	3		5	4	7	8	9	10	11					6		15
1	2	3		5	4	7	8	9	10	11					6		16
1	2	3		5	4	7	8	9	10	11					6		17
1	2	3		5	4	7	8	9	10	11					6		18
1	2	3		5	4	7	8	9*	10	11		12			6		19
1	2	3		5	4	7	8	9	10	11					6		20
1	2	3	6	5	4	7	8	9	10	11							21
1	2	3	4	5	6	7	8	9	10	11							22
1	2	3	6	5	4	7	8	9	10	11*	12						23
1	2		6	5	4	7	8	9	10				3	11			24
1	2	6*		5	4	7	8	9	10	11			3	12			25
	2	6*			4	7	8	9	10	11		12	3	5		1	26
	2			5	4	7	8	9	10	6	11*		3	12		1	27
1	2	3		5	4	7	8	9	10	11			6				28
1	2	6		5	4	7	8	9	10	11			3				29
1	2	3		5	4	7	8	9	10	11			6				30
1	2	3		5	4	7	8	9	10	11	12		6*				31
1	2	3	6	5	4	7	8	9	10	11							32
1	2	3	6*	5	4	7	8	9	10	11			12				33
1	2	3	4*	5	6	7	8	9	10	11			12				34
1	2	3	6*	5	4	7	8	9	10	11			12				35
1	2	3		5	4	7	8	9	10	11			6				36
1	2	3		5	4	7	8	9	10	11			6				37
1	2	3		5	4	7	8*	9	10	11			6	12			38
1	2	3		5	4	7	8	9	10	11			6				39
1	2	3	12	5	4	7	8	9*	10	11			6				40
1	2	3		5	4	7	8		10	11	9		6				41
1	2	3*	12	5	4	7	8		10	11	9		6				42
40	42	34	15	40	42	42	42	36	42	41	6	1	20	3	14	2	
			2								2	6	3	3			
	1			4		7	15	8	19	4	1		2		1		

1975-76

1	Aug	16	(h)	Chelsea	W	2-1	Robson, Longhorn	28,689
2		19	(a)	Bristol C	L	0-3		12,199
3		23	(a)	Oxford U	D	1-1	Moncur	9,069
4		26	(h)	Fulham	W	2-0	Holden, Gibb	25,450
5		30	(h)	Blackpool	W	2-0	Towers 2	24,000
6	Sep	6	(a)	Plymouth A	L	0-1		18,304
7		13	(h)	West Brom A	W	2-0	Halom, Hughes	25,159
8		20	(a)	Blackburn R	W	1-0	Towers	15,773
9		23	(h)	Carlisle U	W	3-2	Robson, Towers (pen), Hughes	28,185
10		27	(h)	Notts Co	W	4-0	Robson 2, Kerr, Halom	27,565
11	Oct	4	(a)	Portsmouth	D	0-0		13,098
12		11	(h)	Orient	W	3-1	Towers (pen), Hughes, Robson	24,327
13		18	(a)	Bristol R	L	0-1		13,577
14		25	(h)	Luton T	W	2-0	Kerr, Robson	28,338
15	Nov	1	(a)	York C	W	4-1	Hughes 2, Hunter (og), Towers (pen)	15,232
16		8	(h)	Nottingham F	W	3-0	Robson, Halom 2	31,227
17		15	(a)	Charlton A	W	2-1	Holden 2	22,307
18		22	(h)	Bristol R	D	1-1	Kerr	31,356
19		29	(h)	Oldham A	W	2-0	Robson 2	28,220
20	Dec	6	(a)	Southampton	L	0-4		17,598
21		13	(h)	Oxford U	W	1-0	Porterfield	22,051
22		20	(a)	Chelsea	L	0-1		22,802
23		26	(h)	Hull C	W	3-1	Holden, Finney, Henderson	32,210
24		27	(a)	Bolton W	L	1-2	Dunne (og)	42,680
25	Jan	10	(a)	West Brom A	D	0-0		25,399
26		17	(h)	Plymouth A	W	2-1	Holden, Kerr	29,737
27	Feb	7	(a)	Fulham	L	0-2		12,839
28		21	(h)	Charlton A	W	4-1	Holden, Moncur, Robson, Towers	30,173
29		24	(a)	Carlisle U	D	2-2	Towers (pen), Holden	20,001
30		28	(a)	Luton T	L	0-2		15,338
31	Mar	13	(a)	Orient	W	2-0	Kerr 2	7,954
32		17	(a)	Nottingham F	L	1-2	Holden	16,995
33		20	(a)	Oldham A	D	1-1	Hughes	13,704
34		23	(h)	Bristol C	D	1-1	Holden	38,395
35		27	(h)	Southampton	W	3-0	Greenwood 2, Holden	34,946
36		30	(h)	York C	W	1-0	Kerr	33,462
37	Apr	3	(a)	Notts Co	D	0-0		14,811
38		10	(h)	Blackburn R	W	3-0	Holden, Parkes (og), Robson	33,523
39		17	(a)	Hull C	W	4-1	Robson, Rowell (og), Dobson (og), Holden	21,296
40		19	(h)	Bolton W	W	2-1	Towers (pen), Robson	51,983
41		20	(a)	Blackpool	L	0-1		16,768
42		24	(h)	Portsmouth	W	2-0	Bolton, Hughes	40,515

FINAL LEAGUE POSITION: 1st in Division Two

Appearances

Sub. Appearances

Goals

Swinburne	Ashurst	Bolton	Longhorn	Clarke	Moncur	Kerr	Gibb	Halom	Robson	Porterfield	Holden	Montgomery	Malone	Towers	Hughes	Henderson	Rowell	Finney	Mitchell	Greenwood	Train	#
1	2	3	4	5	6	7	8*	9	10	11	12											1
1	2	3	4	5	6	7	12	9	10	11*	8											2
		3		5	6	7	4	9	10	12	8*	1	2	11								3
		3		5	6	7	8	12	10	11	9*	1	2	4								4
		3		5	6	7*	4	12	6	10	8	1	2	11								5
		3		5	6	7	4	8	10	12	9*	1	2	11								6
		3	4	5	6	7		8	10	11	9*	1	2		12							7
		3		5	6	7		9	10	11		1	2	4	8							8
		3		5	6	7		9	10	11		1	2	4	8							9
		3		5	6	7		9	10	11		1	2	4	8							10
		3		5	6	7		9	10	11		1	2	4	8							11
	6	3		5		7			10	11	9	1	2	4	8							12
		3		5	6	7*		9	10	11	12	1	2	4	8							13
	3			5	6	7		9	10	11	12	1	2	4*	8							14
				5	6	7		9	10	11		1	2	4	8	3						15
				5	6	7		9	10	11		1	2	4	8	3						16
				5	6	7		9	10	11	12	1	2	4	8*	3						17
				5	6	7		9	10	11	8	1	2	4		3						18
				5	6	7		9	10	11	8	1	2	4		3						19
	12			5	6	7		9	10	11*	8	1	2	4		3						20
			10	5	6	7		9		11	8*	1	2	4		3	12					21
		3		5	6	7		9	10	11*	12	1	2	4				8				22
		3		5	6	7			10	9		1	2	4		11		8*	12			23
	6	3		5		7			10	9		1	2	4		11		8				24
	6	3		5		7			10	9		1	2	4	8*			12		11		25
		3	4	5	6	7*		9	10		8	1	2			12				11		26
		3	12	5	6		8*		10	9		1	2	4				7		11		27
	8*	3		5	6	7			10	9		1	2	4				11		12		28
	8	3		5	6	7			10	9		1	2	4				11				29
	8	3		5	6	7			10	9		1	2	4				11*		12		30
		3	12	5	6	7			10	9		1	2	4*						11	8	31
	5	3	4*	5	6	7			10	9		1	2			12				11	8	32
	5	3			6	7	12			9*		1	2	10	4					11	8	33
	5	3			6	7			10	9		1	2	8						11	4	34
	5	3			6	7			10	9		1	2	4						11	8	35
	5	3			6	7			10*	9		1	2	4	12					11	8	36
	5	3			6	7			10	9		1	2	4						11	8	37
	5	3			6	7			10	9		1	2	4						11	8	38
	5	3			6	7			10	9		1	2				8			11	4	39
	5	3			6	7			10	9		1	2	4	12					11*	8	40
1	5	3			6				10	9*				4		11	2	7		12	8	41
1	5	3			6	7			10	9			2	8	11						4	42
4	20	34	6	31	39	40	5	21	40	20	31	38	39	34	14	11	3	7		13	12	
	1		2			1	3			2	5				3	2	1	1	1	1	3	
		1	1	2	7	1	4	13	1	12				9	7	1	1		1	2		

23

1976-77

1	Aug	21	(a)	Stoke C	D	0-0		27,424
2		24	(h)	Leicester C	D	0-0		36,668
3		28	(h)	Arsenal	D	2-2	Robson, Holden	41,211
4	Sep	4	(a)	Bristol C	L	1-4	Robson	20,593
5		11	(a)	Middlesbrough	L	1-2	Greenwood	29,000
6		18	(h)	Manchester C	L	0-2		37,395
7		25	(a)	West Ham U	D	1-1	Bolton	24,319
8	Oct	2	(h)	Everton	L	0-1		34,670
9		16	(h)	Aston Villa	L	0-1		31,578
10		23	(a)	Queen's Park R	L	0-2		22,408
11		30	(a)	Coventry C	W	2-1	Lee, Hughes	17,184
12	Nov	6	(h)	Liverpool	L	0-1		39,956
13		10	(a)	Manchester U	D	3-3	Lee 2, Hughes	42,685
14		20	(h)	Tottenham H	W	2-1	Train, Lee	30,324
15		23	(a)	Ipswich T	L	1-3	Hughes (pen)	24,605
16		27	(a)	Derby Co	L	0-1		25,423
17	Dec	11	(a)	Birmingham C	L	0-2		24,597
18		18	(h)	Norwich C	L	0-1		23,468
19		27	(a)	Newcastle U	L	0-2		48,400
20		29	(h)	Leeds U	L	0-1		26,999
21	Jan	1	(a)	Liverpool	L	0-2		44,687
22		3	(h)	Coventry C	L	0-1		24,942
23		15	(a)	Leicester C	L	0-2		16,051
24		22	(h)	Stoke C	D	0-0		22,901
25	Feb	5	(a)	Arsenal	D	0-0		30,925
26		11	(h)	Bristol C	W	1-0	Holden	21,407
27		19	(h)	Middlesbrough	W	4-0	Lee, Holden, Arnott, Rowell	33,205
28		22	(h)	West Brom A	W	6-1	Lee 3, Elliott, Holden, Rowell	30,317
29	Mar	5	(h)	West Ham U	W	6-0	Holden 2, Rowell 2, Kerr, Lee	35,357
30		9	(a)	Manchester C	L	0-1		44,439
31		19	(h)	Ipswich T	W	1-0	Waldron	35,376
32		23	(a)	Aston Villa	L	1-4	Holden	34,458
33	Apr	2	(h)	Queen's Park R	W	1-0	Lee	27,550
34		8	(h)	Newcastle U	D	2-2	Arnott, Lee	46,056
35		9	(a)	Leeds U	D	1-1	Lee	32,966
36		11	(h)	Manchester U	W	2-1	Arnott, Towers (pen)	38,785
37		16	(a)	Tottenham H	D	1-1	Holden	34,185
38		23	(h)	Derby Co	D	1-1	Towers (pen)	35,490
39		30	(a)	West Brom A	W	3-2	Towers 2 (1 pen), Lee	27,072
40	May	7	(h)	Birmingham C	W	1-0	Holden	34,193
41		14	(a)	Norwich C	D	2-2	Rowell, Kerr	27,787
42		19	(a)	Everton	L	0-2		36,075

FINAL LEAGUE POSITION: 20th in Division One

Appearances

Sub. Appearances

Goals

Montgomery	Malone	Bolton	Towers	Clarke	Moncur	Kerr	Ashurst	Hughes	Robson	Train	Holden	Greenwood	Swinburne	Longhorn	Rowell	Holton	Foggon	Lee	Siddall	Henderson	Gibb	Brown	Gilbert	Docherty	Elliott	Waldron	Collins	Coady	
1	2	3	4	5	6	7	8	9	10	11																			1
1	2	3	4	5	6	7*	12	8	10	11	9																		2
1	2	3	4	5	6	7		8	10	11	9*	12																	3
		3	4	5	6	7	2	9	10	8		11	1		.														4
		3		5	6	7*	2		10	11	8	9	1	4	12														5
1	2	3	4	5			6	8	10	11		9			7														6
1		3	4	5			2	8*	10	7		9			12	6	11												7
1		3	4	5			2	8	10	11*		12				6	7	9											8
		3	4	5		7	2	9*		12				8		6	10	11	1										9
		3	4	5			2			10		8			7*	6	11	9	1	12									10
	2	3	4	5		12		8*		10		11				6	7	9	1										11
	2	3	4	5				8		10		7				6	11	9	1										12
	2	3	4	5		7*		8		10		11				6	12	9	1										13
		3	4*	5		7		8		10		11			12	6		9	1	2									14
		3		5		7		8		10		11*			4	6		9	1	2	12								15
		3		5		7		8		10					4	6		9	1	2	11								16
		3	4	5		7		8		10		11			12	6		9*	1	2									17
	2	3	4	5		7		8							12	6	11*	9	1			10							18
	2	3	4	5		7		8							11	6		9*	1			10	12						19
		3		5		7*		8		4		11			9	6			1	2	12	10							20
		3		5			4			7		11*			9	6	12		1	2	8	10							21
		3		5		7	6	12		8	9	11*			4				1	2	12	8	10	2					22
		3		5		7	4				9				8		10*		1		12			2	6	11			23
		3	4	5		7	6				10				11*			9	1		12			2		8			24
		3		5		7	6				9				11			10	1		12			2*	4	8			25
		3	4*	5		7	6				9				11			10	1	2					8	12			26
		3	5*			7	6				9				11			10	1		12			2	8	4			27
		3				7	6				9				11			10	1	5				2	8	4			28
		3				7	6				9				11			10	1		12			2	8*	4	5		29
		3				7	6				9				11			10	1		12			2	8	4*	5		30
		3				7	6				10				11			9	1					2	8	4	5		31
		3				7	6				9							10	1					2	8	4	5	11	32
		3				7	6				9				11			10	1					2	8	4*	5	12	33
		3				7	6				9				11			10	1					2	5	4	8		34
		3	4				6				10				11			9	1					2	8	7		5	35
		3	7				6				9				11			10	1					2	8	4*	5	12	36
		3	7				6				9				11			10	1					2	8	4	5		37
		3	7				6				9				11			10	1					2	8	4	5		38
		3	4				6				9				11			10	1					2	7	8	5		39
		3	7			12	6				9				11			10	1					2*	8	4	5		40
		3	7*			12	6				9				11			10	1					2	8	4	5		41
		3				7	6				9				11			10	1					2	8	4	5		42
6	9	42	25	27	5	28	30	18	8	19	24	14	2	2	27	15	7	32	34	8	2	5		20	19	19	12	2	1
			3			1	1	1			1			2	5			1	1	1	2	6	1		1		1	1	
		1	4			2		3	2	1	9	1			5			13						1	3	1			

25

1977-78

#		Date		H/A	Opponent	Result	Score	Scorers	Attendance
1	Aug	20	(a)	Hull C	L	0-3		16,189
2		23	(h)	Burnley	W	3-0	Holden 2, Stevenson (og)	31,405
3		27	(h)	Orient	D	1-1	Ashurst (pen)	28,261
4	Sep	3	(a)	Sheffield U	D	1-1	Lee	17,994
5		10	(a)	Crystal Palace	D	2-2	Rowell, Rostron	21,305
6		17	(h)	Bolton W	L	0-2		30,342
7		24	(a)	Stoke C	D	0-0		18,820
8	Oct	1	(h)	Brighton & HA	L	0-2		24,013
9		4	(h)	Cardiff C	D	1-1	Greenwood	18,484
10		8	(a)	Southampton	L	2-4	Rowell, Lee	17,696
11		15	(h)	Millwall	W	2-0	Arnott, Rowell	22,181
12		22	(a)	Mansfield T	W	2-1	Roston 2	12,827
13		29	(h)	Oldham A	W	3-1	Elliott, Ashurst, Lee	24,712
14	Nov	5	(a)	Fulham	D	3-3	Greenwood, Rowell, Arnott	10,548
15		12	(h)	Bristol R	W	5-1	Arnott, Greenwood, Henderson, Elliott, Lee	24,633
16		19	(a)	Notts Co	D	2-2	Kerr, Rostron	12,247
17		26	(h)	Luton T	D	1-1	Bolton	26,915
18	Dec	3	(a)	Charlton A	L	2-3	Greenwood, Entwistle	12,761
19		10	(h)	Tottenham H	L	1-2	Rowell (pen)	31,960
20		17	(a)	Bristol R	L	2-3	Lee, Rowell (pen)	6,516
21		26	(h)	Blackpool	W	2-1	Rowell 2 (1 pen)	30,628
22		27	(a)	Blackburn R	D	1-1	Gilbert	22,860
23		31	(a)	Burnley	D	0-0		12,649
24	Jan	2	(h)	Hull C	W	2-0	Rowell 2	29,456
25		14	(a)	Orient	D	2-2	Clarke, Rowell	6,737
26		21	(h)	Sheffield U	W	5-1	Kerr, Rostron, Elliott, Rowell 2 (1 pen)	22,634
27		28	(a)	Cardiff C	L	2-5	Clarke, Rowell (pen)	8,459
28	Feb	25	(a)	Brighton & HA	L	1-2	Clarke	25,771
29	Mar	4	(h)	Southampton	D	0-0		20,975
30		7	(a)	Bolton W	L	0-2		20,972
31		14	(h)	Crystal Palace	D	0-0		15,962
32		18	(h)	Mansfield T	W	1-0	Lee	14,033
33		24	(a)	Oldham A	D	1-1	Lee	10,086
34		25	(h)	Blackburn R	L	0-1		16,900
35		27	(a)	Blackpool	D	1-1	Docherty	9,872
36	Apr	1	(h)	Fulham	D	2-2	Docherty, Lee	11,951
37		4	(h)	Stoke C	W	1-0	Kerr	11,151
38		8	(a)	Luton T	W	3-1	Lee, Rowell, Gregoire	7,616
39		15	(h)	Notts Co	W	3-1	Rostron, Kerr, Lee	14,673
40		18	(a)	Millwall	L	1-3	Rowell	7,258
41		22	(a)	Tottenham H	W	3-2	Rowell, Lee 2	38,220
42		29	(h)	Charlton A	W	3-0	Bolton 2, Rowell	16,718

FINAL LEAGUE POSITION: 6th in Division Two

Appearances

Sub. Appearances

Goals

Siddall	Docherty	Bolton	Arnott	Waldron	Ashurst	Kerr	Elliott	Holden	Lee	Rowell	Rostron	Brown	Collins	Henderson	Stronach	Greenwood	Armstrong	Entwistle	Clarke	Gibert	Gregoire	Hindmarch	Weir	No.
1	2	3	4	5	6	7*	8	9	10	11	12													1
1	2	3	4	5	6		8	9	10	11	7													2
1	2	3	4	5*	6		8	10		9	7	11	12											3
1	2	3		5	6	7	8	9	10	4	11								.					4
1	2	3		5	6	7	8		9	10	11			4										5
1	2	3		5	6	12	8		10	11	7	9			4*									6
1	2	3		5	6	12	8	9	10	4	7	11*												7
1	2*	3		5	6		8	9	10	11	7	4						12						8
1		3	8		6	4	5		10*	11	7			2		9	12							9
1		3	8		6	4	5	12	10	11	7			2		9*								10
1		3	4		6	7	5		10	11	8			2		9								11
1		3	8		6	4	5		10	11	7			2		9								12
1		3	4		6	7	5		10	11	8			2		9								13
1		3	4		6	7	5		10	11	8			2		9								14
1		3	8		6	4	5		10	11	7			2		9								15
1		3	8		6	4	5		10	11	7			2		9								16
1		3	8		6	4	5		10	11	7			2		9								17
1		3	8		6	4	5*			11	7			2		9		10	12					18
1		3	8*		6	4	12			11	7			2		9		10	5					19
1		3	8*		6	4	12			11	7			2		9		10	5					20
1		3	8		6	4	12			11	7*			2		9		10	5					21
1	5		8		6	4	12			11	7			2		9		10*	3					22
1	5	3	8		6	7	12			11	10			2		9*			4					23
1	5	3	8		6	12		9*		11				2					10	4	7			24
1						4	8	10	9	11	7			3					5	2	6			25
1					6	4	8	9	10	11	7			2					5	3				26
1						4	8	9	10	11	7			2					5	3	6			27
1	11				6	4	8		10		7			2				9*	5	3	12			28
1	10	2			4	6	9*		11	7	8			12					5	3				29
1	10	2			4	8			11	9	7						12		5	3		6*		30
1	6				7	4	8		10	11	9*			2			12		5	3				31
1	6	3			7	4	12		9	11				2			8		5	10*				32
1	10	3	8		6	4			9					2			7		5	11				33
1	11	3	8*		6	7			9	12				2			10		5	4				34
1	10	3			6	4			9	11				2			7		5	8				35
1	10	3			6	4			9	8				2			7		5	11				36
1	8	3			6	4			9	11	10*			2			7		5	12				37
1	10	2			6	4			9	7	11							8*	5	3				38
1	10	3			6	4	8		9		7			2			12		5	11*				39
1	10	3			6	4			9	11	7			2					5	8				40
1	10	3			6	4	12		9	11	7			2					5	8*				41
1	10	3			6	4	12		9	11	7*			2					5	8				42
42	26	36	21	8	38	36	25	11	32	38	33	6	2	32	2	15	7	7	23	14	5	2	1	
						2	4	2	4	1	1		1		1	4	1		1	3	1	2		
	2	3	3		2	4	3	2	12	18	6			1		4			1	3	1	1		

1978-79

#	Month	Date		Opponent		Score	Scorers	Attendance
1	Aug	19	(h)	Charlton A	W	1-0	Rowell	20,486
2		22	(a)	Orient	L	0-3		7,373
3		26	(a)	Brighton & HA	L	0-2		19,885
4	Sep	2	(h)	Preston NE	W	3-1	Entwistle, Docherty, Greenwood	16,819
5		9	(a)	Crystal Palace	D	1-1	Entwistle	21,112
6		16	(h)	Fulham	D	1-1	Brown	17,976
7		23	(a)	Burnley	W	2-1	Rowell 2 (1 pen)	12,964
8		30	(h)	West Ham U	W	2-1	Rowell 2 (1 pen)	23,676
9	Oct	7	(a)	Sheffield U	L	2-3	Rowell, Lee	18,873
10		14	(h)	Newcastle U	D	1-1	Greenwood	35,405
11		21	(h)	Millwall	W	3-2	Rowell 2, Brown	19,962
12		28	(a)	Oldham A	D	0-0		9,857
13	Nov	4	(h)	Stoke C	L	0-1		25,170
14		11	(a)	Charlton A	W	2-1	Entwistle, Rowell	11,412
15		18	(h)	Brighton & HA	W	2-1	Rowell, Clarke	22,738
16		21	(a)	Preston NE	L	1-3	Elliott	13,204
17		25	(a)	Luton T	W	3-0	Rowell 2, Entwistle	10,249
18	Dec	2	(h)	Bristol R	W	5-0	Entwistle 3, Lee, Rowell	18,864
19		9	(a)	Cardiff C	D	1-1	Rostron	7,178
20		16	(h)	Cambridge U	L	0-2		20,841
21		23	(a)	Notts Co	D	1-1	Entwistle	11,281
22		26	(h)	Leicester C	D	1-1	Clarke	24,544
23	Jan	17	(a)	Blackburn R	D	1-1	Rowell	8,130
24		20	(a)	Fulham	D	2-2	Bolton, Rowell (pen)	11,260
25	Feb	3	(h)	Burnley	W	3-1	Rowell (pen), Rostron, Entwistle	23,030
26		10	(a)	West Ham U	D	3-3	Lee, Rostron 2	24,998
27		24	(a)	Newcastle U	W	4-1	Rowell 3 (1 pen), Rostron, Entwistle	35,000
28	Mar	3	(a)	Millwall	W	1-0	Entwistle	7,889
29		7	(h)	Wrexham	W	1-0	Bolton	25,017
30		10	(h)	Oldham A	W	3-0	Rowell (pen), Bolton, Rostron	25,090
31		14	(h)	Crystal Palace	L	1-2	Rostron	34,986
32		24	(h)	Orient	W	1-0	Rowell	21,189
33		27	(a)	Stoke C	W	1-0	Docherty	24,023
34		30	(h)	Luton T	W	1-0	Rostron	23,358
35	Apr	7	(a)	Bristol R	D	0-0		8,003
36		13	(h)	Notts Co	W	3-0	Lee, Brown, Chisholm	34,027
37		14	(a)	Leicester C	W	2-1	Docherty, Brown	20,740
38		16	(h)	Blackburn R	L	0-1		35,005
39		20	(a)	Cambridge U	W	2-0	Lee, Docherty	10,100
40		25	(h)	Sheffield U	W	6-2	Rostron 3 (2 pen), Lee, Brown, Gilbert	29,822
41		28	(h)	Cardiff C	L	1-2	Ashurst	36,526
42	May	5	(a)	Wrexham	W	2-1	Rostron, Brown	19,133

FINAL LEAGUE POSITION: 4th in Division Two

Appearances

Sub. Appearances

Goals

Siddall	Henderson	Bolton	Chisholm	Clarke	Ashurst	Kerr	Rostron	Entwistle	Docherty	Rowell	Lee	Elliott	Gilbert	Brown	Greenwood	Buckley	Coady	Arnott	Watson	Gregoire	Whitworth	#
1	2	3	4	5	6	7	8*	9	10	11	12											1
1	2	3	4*		6	7	10	9	8	11	12	5										2
1	2*			5	6	7	10		8	11	9	4	3	12								3
1	2	3	4					9	8	11		5	6		7	10						4
1	2	3	5	12				9	4	11		6	10		8*	7						5
1	2	3	5					9	4	11		6	10	12	8	7*						6
1	2	3	7				10	9	4	11		6		8*	12		5					7
1		7	5			3		9	4	11	8	6		10			2					8
1		3	4	5		7*		9	10	11	12	6		8			2					9
1	2	3	7*	5				9	4	11	10	6		8	12							10
1	2	3	7*	5				9	4	11	10	6		8	12							11
1	2	3	5					9	4	11	10	6		8		7						12
1	2	3	5					9	4	11	10	6		8*	12	7						13
1	2	3	5				8	9	4	11	10	6				7						14
1	2*	3	4	5			8	9		11	10	6		12		7						15
1	2	3	4*	5			8	9		11	10	6		12		7						16
1	2	3	4	5			8	9		11	10	6				7						17
1	2	3	4	5			8	9		11	10	6				7						18
1	2	3	4	5			8	9		11	10	6				7						19
1	2	3	4*	5			8	9		11	10	6		12		7						20
1	2	3	5				8	9	4	11	10	6				7						21
1	2	3	4*	5			8	9		11	10	6		12		7						22
1	2	3	5				8	9		11	10	6				7		4				23
1	2	3	5				8	9		11	10	6				7		4				24
1	2		5				8	9		11	10	6	3			7		4				25
1	2	7	5				8	9		11	10	6	3					4				26
1	2	3	7	5			8	9	12	11	10	6						4*				27
	2	3	4	5			8	9		11		6				7		10	1			28
1	2	3	7	5			8*	9		11		6				10		4		12		29
1	2	3	7	5			8	9		11		6				10		4				30
1	2	3	7	5			8*	9		11		6		12		10		4				31
1	2	3	5				8	9	4	11	10	6				7						32
1		3	7	5			8	9	4	11		6				10					2	33
1	3*	7	5				11	9	4	10		6		12		8					2	34
1		7	5				11	9*	4	10		6	3	12		8					2	35
1		7			5		8	12	4	11		6	3		9*	10					2	36
1		7			5				4	11		6	3		9	10		8			2	37
1		7			5				4			6	3		7	10		11			2	38
1					5			9	4	11		6	3		9	10		8			2	39
1					5			9	4	11		6	3		9	10		7			2	40
1	3	7*	12	5			10		4	11		6			9			8			2	41
1	3			5			10	12	4	11*		6			9	8		7			2	42
41	30	32	27	33	10	3	34	34	26	32	30	41	12	14	3	30	3	15	1	1	10	
					1	1		2	1	3	1					8	5			1		
		3	1	2	1		11	11	4	21	6	11	6	2								

1979-80

1	Aug	18	(a)	Chelsea	D	0-0		23500
2		22	(h)	Birmingham C	W	2-0	Robson, Brown	25877
3		25	(h)	Fulham	W	2-1	Arnott, Robson (pen)	25506
4	Sep	1	(a)	Oldham A	L	0-3		7830
5		8	(h)	Cambridge U	W	2-0	Buckley, Elliott	22898
6		15	(a)	West Ham U	L	0-2		24021
7		22	(a)	Burnley	D	1-1	Robson	8751
8		29	(h)	Preston NE	D	1-1	Clarke	24594
9	Oct	6	(h)	Charlton A	W	4-0	Hawley 3, Robson	24865
10		9	(a)	Birmingham C	L	0-1		18960
11		13	(a)	Luton T	L	0-2		13504
12		20	(h)	Queen's Park R	W	3-0	Robson 2 (1 pen), Hawley	25201
13		27	(a)	Leicester C	L	1-2	Lee	19365
14	Nov	3	(h)	Chelsea	W	2-1	Arnott, Gilbert	24988
15		10	(a)	Swansea C	L	1-3	Brown	15826
16		17	(h)	Notts Co	W	3-1	Robson 2 (1 pen), Cummins	21896
17		24	(h)	Bristol R	W	3-2	Elliott, Cummins, Robson	21292
18	Dec	1	(a)	Orient	L	1-2	Robson	6582
19		8	(h)	Cardiff C	W	2-1	Davies (og), Robson	25370
20		15	(a)	Watford	D	1-1	Dunn	13965
21		21	(h)	Shrewsbury T	W	2-1	Marangoni, Arnott	21237
22		26	(h)	Wrexham	D	1-1	Arnott	29567
23		29	(a)	Fulham	W	1-0	Marangoni	9591
24	Jan	1	(a)	Newcastle U	L	1-3	Cummins	38332
25		12	(h)	Oldham A	W	4-2	Brown 3, Robson	19456
26		19	(a)	Cambridge U	D	3-3	Marangoni, Brown, Cummins	7107
27	Feb	9	(h)	Burnley	W	5-0	Cummins 4, Arnott	21855
28		16	(a)	Preston NE	L	1-2	Brown	12165
29		23	(h)	Luton T	W	1-0	Cooke	25387
30	Mar	1	(a)	Queen's Park R	D	0-0		15613
31		8	(h)	Leicester C	D	0-0		29487
32		15	(a)	Charlton A	W	4-0	Brown, Arnott, Robson 2	6185
33		22	(h)	Swansea C	D	1-1	Robson	25175
34		29	(a)	Notts Co	W	1-0	Cummins	10878
35	Apr	5	(h)	Newcastle U	W	1-0	Cummins	41752
36		7	(a)	Wrexham	W	1-0	Brown	12064
37		8	(a)	Shrewsbury T	W	2-1	Robson, Cummins	123456
38		12	(h)	Orient	D	1-1	Arnott	33279
39		19	(a)	Bristol R	D	2-2	Robson, Dunn	9757
40		26	(h)	Watford	W	5-0	Robson 2, Buckley, Elliott 2	32195
41	May	3	(a)	Cardiff C	D	1-1	Robson	19340
42		12	(h)	West Ham U	W	2-0	Arnott, Cummins	45000

FINAL LEAGUE POSITION: 2nd in Division Two

Appearances

Sub. Appearances

Goals

Siddall	Whitworth	Bolton	Clarke	Elliott	Chisholm	Arnott	Rostron	Rowell	Robson	Brown	Entwistle	Buckley	Ashurst	Lee	Turner	Gilbert	Dunn	Hawley	Hindmarch	Hughes	Cummins	Cooke	Marangoni	Coady	Hinnigan	
1	2	3	4	5	6	7	8	9	10	11																1
1	2	3	4	5	6	7	8	9	10	11																2
1	2	3	4	5	6	7	8		10	11	9															3
1	2	3	4	5	6	7*	8		10	11	9	12														4
1	2	3	4	5			8	11	10	9		7	6													5
1	2	3	4	5*	12	11	8		10	9		6	7													6
1	2	3*	4	5	6			11	10	9		7	12	8												7
	2		4	5	6	10	11*			9		7		8	1	3	12									8
	2		4	5	6	7			10					8	1	3	11	9								9
	2		4	5		7			10					8	1	3	11	9	6							10
	2		4	5		7			10			12		8	1	3	11*	9	6							11
1	2	5	4			7*			10			12		8		3	11	9	6							12
1	2		4	5		7		12	10					8		3	11	9*	6							13
1	2	3	4	5		7		12	10*	9						8	11		6							14
	2	3	4	5	11	7			10	9					1	8				6						15
	2	3	4	5		7		12	10	9*		6			1		11				8					16
	2	3	4	5		7			10			6			1		11				8	9				17
	2	3	4	5		7			10	12		6			1		11	9*			8					18
	2	3	4	5		7			10	9		6			1						8		11			19
	2	3	4	5		7			10	9		6*			1		12				8		11			20
	2	3	4	5		7		12	10	9*		6			1						8		11			21
	2	3	4	5		7		12	10	9		6			1						8		11*			22
	2	3	4	5		7		11	10	12		6			1			9*			8					23
	2	3	4	5		7		12	10*			6			1			9			8		11			24
1	2	3	4	5		7		12	10	9		6					11*				8					25
1	2	3	4	5		7			10	9		6					11				8					26
	2	3	4	6		7			10	9					1				5		11		8			27
	2	3	4	6		7			10	9*					1				5		11		8	12		28
	2		4	6*		7		12	10	9									5		11		8		3	29
	2		4	6		7			10	9									5		11		8		3	30
	2		4	6		7		12	10	9									5		11		8*		3	31
	2		4	6		7		12	10	9*									5		11		8		3	32
	2		4	6		7			10	9									5		11		8		3	33
	2		4	6		7		12	10	9									5		11		8*		3	34
	2		4	6		7		8	10	9									5		11				3	35
	2		4	6		7			10	9								8	5		11				3	36
	2			6		7			10	9								8	5		11				3	37
	2		6	4		7			10	9		12			1			8*	5		11				3	38
	2		4			7			10	9		6			1			8	5		11				3	39
	2		4	6		7			10	9					1			8	5		11				3	40
	2		4*	6		7			10	9					1		12		5		11				3	41
	2		6	4		7			10	8					1			9	5		11				3	42
12	42	22	39	41	12	37	8	8	40	29	2	17	2	7	30	8	15	9	21	1	26	4	16		14	
				1						9		4		2	1		5							1		
		1	4		8				20	9		2		1	1		2				12	1	3			

31

1980-81

#	Month	Date		Opponent	Result	Score	Scorers	Attendance
1	Aug	16	(h)	Everton	W	3-1	Hawley (pen), Cummins, Lyons (og)	32,005
2		20	(a)	Manchester C	W	4-0	Cummins, Hawley 3 (1 pen)	33,271
3		23	(h)	Southampton	L	1-2	Allardyce	41,141
4		30	(a)	Manchester U	D	1-1	Brown	51,498
5	Sep	6	(a)	Leicester C	W	1-0	Hawley	20,638
6		13	(h)	Middlesbrough	L	0-1		32,745
7		20	(a)	Tottenham H	D	0-0		32,030
8		27	(h)	Leeds U	W	4-1	Robson 2, Rowell, Brown	29,619
9	Oct	4	(a)	Aston Villa	L	0-4		26,914
10		8	(h)	Nottingham F	D	2-2	Rowell, Brown	30,515
11		11	(h)	Crystal Palace	W	1-0	Rowell	25,444
12		18	(a)	Arsenal	D	2-2	Rowell, Cummins	32,135
13		21	(a)	Coventry C	L	1-2	Cummins	13,115
14		25	(h)	Ipswich T	L	0-2		32,368
15	Nov	1	(a)	Wolves	L	1-2	Allardyce	18,816
16		8	(h)	Stoke C	D	0-0		21,483
17		12	(h)	Manchester C	W	2-0	Arnott, Cooke	23,387
18		15	(a)	Everton	L	1-2	Robson	24,099
19		22	(a)	Norwich C	L	0-1		15,024
20		29	(h)	Liverpool	L	2-4	Brown, Cummins	32,340
21	Dec	6	(a)	Brighton & HA	L	1-2	Chisholm	13,903
22		13	(h)	Arsenal	W	2-0	Hawley, Arnott	21,595
23		20	(a)	Nottingham F	L	1-3	Rowell	23,151
24		26	(h)	West Brom A	D	0-0		28,296
25		27	(a)	Birmingham C	L	2-3	Hawley, Rowell	19,005
26	Jan	10	(h)	Norwich C	W	3-0	Rowell 2, Cummins	17,749
27		28	(h)	Manchester U	W	2-0	Chisholm, Rowell (pen)	31,910
28		31	(a)	Southampton	L	1-2	Chisholm	21,345
29	Feb	7	(a)	Middlesbrough	L	0-1		35,065
30		14	(h)	Leicester C	W	1-0	Cummins	22,569
31		21	(a)	Leeds U	L	0-1		23,236
32		28	(h)	Tottenham H	D	1-1	Bowyer	22,382
33	Mar	7	(h)	Aston Villa	L	1-2	Hinnigan	27,278
34		14	(a)	Crystal Palace	W	1-0	Hinnigan	16,748
35		21	(h)	Coventry C	W	3-0	Hinnigan 2, Cummins (pen)	20,622
36		28	(a)	Ipswich T	L	1-4	Rowell	25,450
37	Apr	4	(h)	Wolves	L	0-1		20,138
38		11	(a)	Stoke C	L	0-2		11,501
39		18	(h)	Birmingham C	W	3-0	Ritchie 3 (1 pen)	20,158
40		20	(a)	West Brom A	L	1-2	Ritchie (pen)	15,243
41		25	(h)	Brighton & HA	L	1-2	Brown	22,317
42	May	2	(a)	Liverpool	W	1-0	Cummins	40,337

FINAL LEAGUE POSITION: 17th in Division One

Appearances

Sub. Appearances

Goals

Turner	Whitworth	Bolton	Allardyce	Elliott	Hindmarch	Arnott	Buckley	Hawley	Brown	Cummins	Chisholm	Robson	Himnigan	Marangoni	Rowell	Dunn	Cooke	Bowyer	Siddall	Ritchie	Vincent	
1	2	3	4	5	6	7	8	9	10	11												1
1	2	3	4	5	6		8*	9	10	11	7	12										2
1	2	3	4	5	6		8*	9	10	11	7	12										3
1		3	4	5		8		9	10	11	7		2	6								4
1		3	4	5		8		9	10	11	7		2	6								5
1		3	4	5		8		9*	10	11	7		2	6	12							6
1		3	4	5		7			10	11	6	9	2*		8	12						7
1	2	3	4	5		7			10	11	6	9			8							8
1	2	3	4	5		7			9	11	6*	10			8	12						9
1	2	3	4	5		7			10	11	6	9			8							10
1	2	3	4	5		7			10	11	6	9			8							11
1	2	3	4	5		7			10	11	6				8		9					12
1	2	3	4	5		7			10	11	6				8		9					13
1	2	3	4	5		7			10	11	6				8		9					14
1	2	3	4	5		7		6	10	11					8		9					15
1	2	3	4	5		7		6	10*	11	12				8		9					16
1	2	3		5*	4	7		6		11		10		12	8		9					17
1	2	3	5		4	7		6		11		10			8		9					18
1	2	3	4		5	7		6	12	11	10*					8	9					19
1	2	3	5	6	4	7			8	11	12	10					9*					20
1	2	3	5	6	4	7			8*	11	10				12		9					21
1	2	3	5	6	4	7		9	8*	11	10						12					22
1	2	3	5		4	7		9	8*	11	10				6		12					23
1	2	3	5		4	7		9	12	11*	10				6		8					24
1	2	3	5		4	7		9		11	10				6		8					25
1	2	3	5		4	7		9	8	11	10				6							26
1	2	3	5		4	7		9*	12	11	10				6			8				27
	2	3	5		4	7*		9		11	10				6			8	1	12		28
	2	3	5		4			9		11	10				6			8	1	7		29
	2		5		4			9		11	10	3			6			8	1	7		30
	2		5		4			9	12	11	10	3			6*			8	1	7		31
	2		5		4	7			12	11	10*	3			6			8	1	9		32
		3	5		4	7				11	10	2			6		12	8*	1	9		33
		3	5		4	7		6	12	11	10	2					8*		1	9		34
		3	5		4	7		6		11	10	2					8		1	9		35
		3	5		4	7		6	8	11		2			12			10	1	9*		36
	2	3	5		4	7			8*	11	6				12			10	1	9		37
		3	5		4	7			8	11	6	2			10				1	9		38
		3	5	6*	4	7	8		10	11		2			12				1	9		39
		3	5		4		8		10	11	7	2							1	9	6	40
		3	5		4		8		10*	11	7	2			6				1	9	12	41
		3	12	5	4		8		10	11	7*	2			6				1	9		42
27	29	39	24	38	29	34	15	16	28	42	33	9	16	3	26	1	14	9	15	14	1	
			1						6		1	3		1	5	2	3			1	1	
		2				2	7	5	9	3	3	4			10		1	1		4		

33

1981-82

1	Aug	29	(a)	Ipswich T	D	3-3	Ritchie, Buckley 2	24,060
2	Sep	2	(h)	Aston Villa	W	2-1	Ritchie, Rowell	29,372
3		5	(h)	West Ham U	L	0-2		28,347
4		12	(a)	Arsenal	D	1-1	Rowell	26,471
5		19	(h)	Wolves	D	0-0		22,061
6		23	(a)	Nottingham F	L	0-2		21,133
7		26	(a)	Swansea C	L	0-2		17,826
8	Oct	3	(h)	Coventry C	D	0-0		19,269
9		10	(a)	Notts Co	L	0-2		10,683
10		17	(h)	Tottenham H	L	0-2		25,317
11		24	(a)	Leeds U	L	0-1		25,220
12		31	(h)	Liverpool	L	0-2		27,854
13	Nov	7	(h)	Manchester U	L	1-5	Cummins	27,070
14		14	(a)	Middlesbrough	D	0-0		21,019
15		21	(a)	Everton	W	2-1	Ritchie (pen), Elliott	19,759
16		25	(h)	Nottingham F	L	2-3	Hindmarch, McCoist	17,419
17		28	(h)	West Brom A	L	1-2	Hindmarch	15,867
18	Dec	5	(a)	Brighton & HA	L	1-2	Ritchie	14,251
19		19	(a)	Manchester C	W	3-2	Cummins, Rowell, Venison	29,462
20	Jan	30	(a)	Wolves	W	1-0	Cooke	11,099
21	Feb	2	(a)	Aston Villa	L	0-1		19,916
22		6	(h)	Arsenal	D	0-0		16,345
23		10	(h)	Stoke C	L	0-2		14,317
24		16	(a)	Birmingham C	L	0-2		10,776
25		20	(h)	Swansea C	L	0-1		13,163
26		27	(h)	Notts Co	D	1-1	Brown	12,910
27	Mar	10	(h)	Southampton	W	2-0	Pickering, McCoist	15,747
28		13	(h)	Leeds U	L	0-1		20,285
29		20	(a)	Liverpool	L	0-1		30,344
30		27	(a)	Manchester U	D	0-0		40,776
31	Apr	3	(h)	Middlesbrough	L	0-2		19,006
32		7	(h)	Ipswich T	D	1-1	West	11,845
33		10	(a)	Stoke C	W	1-0	Buckley	11,399
34		12	(h)	Birmingham C	W	2-0	West 2	14,821
35		14	(a)	Tottenham H	D	2-2	Rowell (pen), Pickering	39,898
36		17	(h)	Everton	W	3-1	Rowell 2 (1 pen), West	18,359
37		24	(a)	West Brom A	W	3-2	Cummins, Pickering, Rowell	13,268
38		27	(a)	Coventry C	L	1-6	Cummins	11,227
39	May	1	(h)	Brighton & HA	W	3-0	Rowell 2 (1 pen), West	16,224
40		4	(a)	West Ham U	D	1-1	West	17,130
41		8	(a)	Southampton	L	0-1		21,110
42		15	(h)	Manchester C	W	1-0	Buckley	26,167

FINAL LEAGUE POSITION: 19th in Division One

Appearances

Sub. Appearances

Goals

#	Turner	Hinnigan	Munro	Buckley	Clarke	Hindmarch	Chisholm	Ritchie	Brown	Rowell	Pickering	McCoist	Cooke	Siddall	Elliott	Arnott	Cummins	Whitworth	Venison	West	Bowyer	Nicholl	McGinley	Ursem	#
1	1	2	3	4	5	6	7	8	9*	10	11	12													1
2	1	2	3	4	5	6	7	8		10	11	12	9*												2
3	1	2	3	4	5	6	7	8		10	11*	12	9												3
4		2	3	4	5	6	12	9		10	11	8*		1	7										4
5		2	3	4	5	6		9		10	11	8		1	7										5
6		2	3	4	5	6		9	10*		11	12		1		7	8								6
7		2		4	5	6		9		10	11*	12		1	3	7	8								7
8		2	3	4	5	6		9		10		8		1	7		11								8
9			3		5			9	8*	10	7	12		1	6		11	2	4						9
10					5	6		9		10		8		1	3	7	11	2*	4	12					10
11				4*	5		7	9		10	3	8		1	6		11		2	12					11
12			3	4	5		7	9*		10		8		1	6		11		2	12					12
13			3		5				8	10				1	6	7	11		2	9	4				13
14			3		5	4	7			10	9			1	6		11		2	8					14
15			3	7	5	4	12			10*		8		1	6		11		2	9					15
16			3	7	5	4	12			10		8		1	6		11		2	9					16
17			3	7	5	4		6		10*		8	12	1			11		2	9					17
18			3*	7	5		12	6		10		8		1	4		11		2	9					18
19		2*		7	5	4		9		10	3	8		1	6		11		12						19
20			3	7	5	4	8	12		10		9		1	6		11*		2						20
21			3		5	4	8	7		10*	11	9		1	6				2	12					21
22			3	7		4				10		12	9	1	6		11*		2	5	8				22
23			3	7	5				8*	12	10	9		1	6		4				2	11			23
24			3*	10	7	5	4			12	9			1	6		11			8	2				24
25		2	3	7	5	4				9		8		1	6		11*		12				10		25
26		2	3	7	5	4		9		10	6	12		1			11						8*		26
27	1	2	3	7	4	5				9	10	8			6		11								27
28	1	2*	3	7	4	5				9	10	8			6		11		12						28
29	1	2	3	7	4	5*				9	10	8			6		11		12						29
30	1		3	7	4					9	10	8			6	5	11		2						30
31	1		3	7	4					9	10	8*			6	5	11		2				12		31
32	1	2	3	7	4	5				9	10				6		11			8					32
33	1	2	3	7	4		5			9*	10				6		11			8			12		33
34	1	2	3	7	4					9*	10		5		6		11			8			12		34
35	1	2*	3	7	4	5				9	10				6		11			8			12		35
36	1	2	3	7	4	5				9	10				6		11			8					36
37	1	2	3	7	4	5				9	10				6		11			8					37
38	1	2	3	7	4	5				9	10*	12			6		11			8					38
39	1	2	3	7	4	5				9	10				6		11			8					39
40	1	2	3	7	4	5				9	10				6		11			8					40
41	1	2	3	7	12	4	5			9	10				6		11*			8					41
42	1	2	3	7	4	5				9	10				6		11			8					42
	13	30	34	37	25	36	20	18	5	30	37	19	8	23	36	6	35	2	17	13	6	3	3		
				1			2	2	2			9	2						3	5			4		
			4		2		4	1	9	3	2	1		1			4		1	6					

1982-83

1	Aug	28	(a)	Aston Villa	W	3-1	West, McCoist, Pickering		22,945
2	Sep	1	(h)	Notts Co	D	1-1	Rowell		18,997
3		4	(h)	West Ham U	W	1-0	Rowell		19,239
4		7	(a)	Coventry C	L	0-1			8,190
5		11	(a)	Brighton & HA	L	2-3	Cummins, McCoist		10,264
6		18	(h)	Tottenham H	L	0-1			21,137
7		25	(a)	Watford	L	0-8			16,744
8	Oct	2	(h)	Norwich C	W	4-1	Rowell 2, McCoist, Cooke		13,144
9		9	(h)	Southampton	D	1-1	McCoist		15,635
10		16	(a)	Manchester C	D	2-2	McCoist, Buckley		25,053
11		23	(a)	Everton	L	1-3	McCoist		20,360
12		30	(h)	Stoke C	D	2-2	Pickering, Rowell		16,406
13	Nov	6	(a)	Swansea C	L	0-3			10,034
14		13	(h)	Luton T	D	1-1	Atkins		14,238
15		20	(h)	Nottingham F	L	0-1			14,716
16		27	(a)	Birmingham C	L	1-2	Rowell		12,375
17	Dec	4	(h)	Ipswich T	L	2-3	Atkins, Worthington		15,000
18		11	(a)	West Brom A	L	0-3			11,136
19		18	(h)	Arsenal	W	3-0	Rowell 3		11,753
20		27	(a)	Manchester U	D	0-0			47,763
21		28	(h)	Liverpool	D	0-0			35,041
22	Jan	1	(a)	Nottingham F	D	0-0			20,382
23		3	(a)	Notts Co	W	1-0	Cummins		9,327
24		15	(a)	Aston Villa	W	2-0	McNaught (og), Worthington		16,052
25		22	(a)	Tottenham H	D	1-1	Cummins (pen)		25,250
26	Feb	5	(h)	Coventry C	W	2-1	Cummins, Rowell		14,356
27		19	(a)	Southampton	L	0-2			17,326
28		26	(h)	Manchester C	W	3-2	Atkins, Rowell 2 (pen)		15,144
29	Mar	5	(h)	Everton	W	2-1	Rowell 2 (1 pen)		16,051
30		12	(a)	Stoke C	W	1-0	Rowell		12,806
31		19	(h)	Swansea C	D	1-1	Rowell		17,445
32		26	(a)	Luton T	W	3-1	Pickering 2, James		11,221
33	Apr	2	(a)	Liverpool	L	0-1			35,821
34		4	(h)	Manchester U	D	0-0			31,486
35		9	(a)	West Ham U	L	1-2	Pickering		20,053
36		16	(a)	Norwich C	L	0-2			15,883
37		19	(h)	Brighton & HA	D	1-1	Pickering		13,414
38		23	(a)	Ipswich T	L	1-4	Pickering		16,193
39		30	(h)	Birmingham C	L	1-2	West		14,818
40	May	2	(h)	Watford	D	2-2	Atkins, James		13,971
41		7	(a)	Arsenal	W	1-0	West		18,053
42		14	(h)	West Brom A	D	1-1	Chisholm		16,376

FINAL LEAGUE POSITION: 16th in Division One

Appearances

Sub. Appearances

Goals

Turner	Venison	Munro	Atkins	Chisholm	Elliott	Buckley	West	McCoist	Pickering	Cummins	Hindmarch	Rowell	Cooke	Hinnigan	Nicholl	Worthington	Prudhoe	James	Proctor	Whitfield	
1	2	3	4	5	6	7	8	9	10	11											1
1	2	3	4		6	7	8	9	10*	11	5	12									2
1	2	3	4		6	7		9	10	11	5	8									3
1	2	3	4	6*		7		9	10	11	5	8	12								4
1	2*	3		6		7		9	10	11	5	8	12	4							5
1	2	3		6		7		9	10*	11	5	8	12	4							6
1	2	3	4			7		9	10	11	5	8			6						7
1	4	3			6	7		9	10		5	8	11		2						8
1		3	4		6	7		9	10		5	8	11		2						9
1	11	3	4	5	6	7		9	10	12		8			2*						10
1	12	3	4	5	6*	7	10	9		11		8			2						11
1	11	3		5		7	10	9	6		4	8			2						12
1	11	3	12	5		7*	10	9	6		4	8			2						13
1	11	3	4	5			10	9	6	7		8			2						14
1	11	3	4	5			10	9	12	6*	7	8			2						15
1		3	4	5	6	7	12		10	11*		8	9		2						16
1		3	4	5		7			10	11	6	8			2	9					17
	2	3	4		6				10			8	11	5	7	9	1				18
1	7	3	4	5	6				10	11		8			2	9					19
1		3	4	5	6	7			10	11		8			2	9					20
1	7		4	5	6*			12	3	11		8	10		2	9					21
1	7		4	5		6	9		3	11		8	10		2						22
1	7		4	5			8	9	3	11	6		10		2						23
1	7	3	4	5			8	12	6	11					2	9*		10			24
1	7	3	4	5			8	12	6	11					2	9*		10			25
1	7	3*	4	5			12		6	11		8			2	9		10			26
1	7	3	4	5			12		6	11*		8			2	9		10			27
1	7	3	4	5					6	11		8			2	9		10			28
1	7	3	4	5			12		6	11		8			2	9		10*			29
1	7	3	4	5			9		6	11		8			2			10			30
1	7		4	5			12		3	11*		8			2	9		10	6		31
1	7	3	4	5						11		9			2	8		10	6		32
1	7	3	4	5			12			11		8			2	9*		10	6		33
1	7	3	4	5					12	11*		8			2	9		10	6		34
1		3		5	4			12	11	7*		8			2	9		10	6		35
1*	7	3	4	5			12	9	11	6		8						10	2		36
	7	3	4	5					6			8	11			9	1	10	2		37
	2	3	4	5			8	12	11		5	7				9*	1	10			38
	7	3	4	5			9		6	11		8					1	10	2		39
	7	3	4	5	2		9	12	6	11		8					1	10*			40
	7	3	4	5	2		9	10	6	11			8				1				41
		3	4	5	2*		9		11	8	6	7				12	1	10			42
35	36	37	36	32	20	18	19	19	39	29	14	34	11	3	29	18	7	18	5	3	
	1		1			2	4	9	1			1	3			1					
		4	1		1	3	6	7	4			16	1			2		2			

1983-84

1	Aug	27	(h)	Norwich C	D	1-1	West	17,057
2		29	(a)	Aston Villa	L	0-1		20,390
3	Sep	3	(a)	Luton T	L	1-4	West	10,846
4		7	(h)	Wolverhampton W	W	3-2	Rowell (pen), Daniel (og), Atkinson	12,961
5		10	(h)	Southampton	L	0-2		12,716
6		17	(a)	QPR	L	0-3		12,929
7		24	(h)	Coventry C	W	1-0	West	11,612
8	Oct	1	(a)	Liverpool	W	1-0	Rowell (pen)	29,534
9		15	(h)	Stoke C	D	2-2	Thomas (og), Rowell	11,793
10		22	(h)	Manchester U	L	0-1		26,826
11		29	(a)	Nottingham F	D	1-1	Rowell	13,968
12	Nov	5	(a)	Arsenal	W	2-1	West, Atkins	26,064
13		12	(h)	Watford	W	3-0	West, Proctor, Chisholm	15,407
14		19	(h)	West Ham U	L	0-1		19,921
15		26	(a)	Birmingham C	W	1-0	Bracewell	11,948
16	Dec	3	(h)	Ipswich T	D	1-1	Rowell	15,555
17		10	(a)	Notts Co	L	1-6	Bracewell	7,123
18		18	(h)	Leicester C	D	1-1	Rowell	16,993
19		26	(a)	Everton	D	0-0		18,683
20		27	(h)	West Brom A	W	3-0	Robson, Bracewell 2	17,968
21		31	(h)	Luton T	W	2-0	Chisholm, Pickering	19,482
22	Jan	2	(a)	Coventry C	L	1-2	West	13,249
23		14	(a)	Norwich C	L	0-3		16,320
24	Feb	4	(h)	Liverpool	D	0-0		25,646
25		8	(a)	Tottenham H	L	0-3		19,327
26		11	(a)	Southampton	D	1-1	Chapman	16,968
27		18	(h)	Nottingham F	D	1-1	Chisholm	15,958
28		25	(a)	Manchester U	L	1-2	Chapman	40,615
29	Mar	3	(h)	Arsenal	D	2-2	Proctor, Rowell (pen)	15,370
30		7	(h)	QPR	W	1-0	Fenwick (og)	13,538
31		17	(a)	Wolverhampton W	D	0-0		9,111
32		20	(a)	Watford	L	1-2	Rowell	16,231
33		24	(h)	Aston Villa	L	0-1		11,908
34		31	(a)	Stoke C	L	1-2	Atkins	11,047
35	Apr	7	(h)	Tottenham H	D	1-1	West	15,433
36		14	(a)	West Ham U	W	1-0	Chisholm	16,558
37		21	(h)	Everton	W	2-1	Robson, West	15,876
38		23	(a)	West Brom A	L	1-3	West	11,252
39		28	(h)	Birmingham C	W	2-1	James 2 (2 pens)	13,061
40	May	5	(a)	Ipswich T	L	0-1		17,657
41		7	(h)	Notts Co	D	0-0		14,517
42		12	(a)	Leicester C	W	2-0	Chapman, Robson	12,627

FINAL LEAGUE POSITION: 13th in Division One

Appearances

Sub Appearances

Goals

Turner	Venison	Munro	Atkins	Chisholm	Proctor	Bracewell	Rowell	West	Pickering	Atkinson	Cooke	Elliott	James	Hindmarch	Walker	Robson	Chapman	Murray	No.
1	2	3	4	5	6	7	8	9	10	11									1
1	2	3	4	5	10	6*	8	9	7	11	12								2
1	2	3	4	5	10		8	9	7	11		6							3
1	2	3	4	5	10		8	9	6	11			7*	12					4
1	2	3	4	5	6	7	8	9	10	11*			12						5
1	2		4	5	6	7	8	9	10	11		3							6
1	2		4	5	6	7	8	9	10		12	11*	3						7
1	2		4	5	6	7	8	9	10			3	11						8
1	2		4	5	6	7	8	9	10			3	11						9
1	2*		4	5	6	7	8	9	10		12	3	11						10
1	2			5	10	7	8	9	3		11	6		5					11
1	2		4	5	10	7	8	9	3			6	11						12
1	2		4	5	10	7	8	9	3	11*		6	12						13
1	2		4	5	10	7	8	9	3			6	11						14
1	2		4	5	10	7	8	9	3			6	11						15
1	2		4	5	10	7	8	9	3			6	11						16
1	2		4	5	10	7	8	9	3		12	6	11*						17
1	2		4	5	10	7	8	9	3			6	11						18
1	2		4	5	10	7	8	9	3*	11		6	12						19
1	2		4	5	10	7		9	3			6	11			8			20
1	2		4	5	10	7		9	3			6	11*	12		8			21
1		2	4	5	10*	7	11	9	3			6		12		8			22
1	2		4		10	7	8	9	3			6	11	5					23
1	2		4	5	10	7	8	9	3			6	11						24
1	2		4		10	7	8	9	3			6	11			5			25
1	2		4		10	7	8	9	3			6	11			5			26
1	2		4	5	10	7	8		3			6	11				9		27
1	2		4	5	10	7	8	12	3			6	11*				9		28
1	2	7	4	5	10	12	8*		3			6	11				9		29
1	2	7	4	5	10	8*	12		3			6	11				9		30
1	2		4	5	10	7	8		3			6	11				9		31
1	2	6*	4	5	10	7	8		3				11			12	9		32
1	2		4	5	10	7	8*		3			6	11			12	9		33
1	2		4	5	10	7	12	8	3			6	11				9*		34
1	2			5	10	7	8	9	3			6	11			12		4*	35
1	2		4	5		7		9	3			6	11	10		8			36
1	2		4		10	7		9	3			6	11	5		8			37
1	2		4	5*	8	7	12	9	3			6	11	10					38
1	2		4		10	7		9	3			6	11	5		8			39
1	2		4		10*	7	12	9	3			6	11	5		8			40
1	2		4		10	7		9	3			6	11	5		8*	12		41
1	2		4	5	10	7		9	3			6	11			8			42
42	41	9	40	36	40	38	31	36	42	7	1	33	32	12	0	7	14	1	
					1		3	2		1	3		2	1	1	5	1		
		2	4	2	4	8	9	1	1			2				3	3		

39

1984-85

1	Aug	25	(h)	Southampton	W	3-1	Bennett, Proctor, Venison	18,000
2		27	(a)	Chelsea	L	0-1		25,554
3	Sep	1	(a)	Nottingham F	L	1-3	West (pen)	15,760
4		4	(h)	Tottenham H	W	1-0	West (pen)	18,895
5		8	(h)	West Brom A	D	1-1	Berry	18,206
6		15	(a)	Liverpool	D	1-1	Wylde	34,044
7		22	(h)	Coventry C	D	0-0		16,308
8		29	(a)	Stoke C	D	2-2	Gayle, Walker	8,882
9	Oct	6	(a)	Sheffield W	D	2-2	Atkinson, Walker	27,766
10		13	(h)	Norwich C	W	2-1	Gayle, Berry	15,155
11		20	(a)	Arsenal	L	2-3	Walker 2	36,944
12		27	(h)	Luton T	W	3-0	Chisholm, Pickering, Wylde (pen)	15,280
13	Nov	3	(h)	QPR	W	3-0	Hodgson, Wicks (og), Wylde	16,408
14		10	(a)	Watford	L	1-3	Hodgson	18,900
15		17	(a)	West Ham U	L	0-1		15,204
16		24	(h)	Manchester U	W	3-2	Walker 3 (2 pens)	25,405
17	Dec	1	(a)	Aston Villa	L	0-1		14,669
18		8	(h)	Leicester C	L	0-4		16,441
19		15	(a)	Ipswich T	W	2-0	Bennett, Walker	12,493
20		23	(h)	Nottingham F	L	0-2		21,086
21		26	(h)	Everton	L	1-2	Proctor	19,714
22		29	(a)	Tottenham H	L	0-2		26,930
23	Jan	1	(a)	Newcastle U	L	1-3	West	36,821
24		29	(a)	Southampton	L	0-1		15,326
25	Feb	2	(h)	Stoke C	W	1-0	Hodgson	14,762
26		23	(a)	QPR	L	0-1		10,063
27	Mar	2	(a)	Luton T	L	1-2	Bennett	8,019
28		9	(h)	Arsenal	D	0-0		27,694
29		12	(h)	Watford	D	1-1	Walker	22,375
30		16	(a)	Norwich C	W	3-1	Downs (og), Hodgson, Wallace	13,389
31		30	(h)	Chelsea	L	0-2		13,489
32	Apr	3	(h)	Liverpool	L	0-3		24,096
33		6	(a)	Everton	L	1-4	Wallace	35,978
34		8	(h)	Newcastle U	D	0-0		28,246
35		13	(a)	Coventry C	W	1-0	Moore	9,668
36		16	(h)	Sheffield W	D	0-0		16,119
37		20	(h)	West Ham U	L	0-1		15,622
38		24	(a)	West Brom A	L	0-1		7,423
39		27	(a)	Manchester U	D	2-2	Pickering, Walker	38,979
40	May	4	(h)	Aston Villa	L	0-4		12,467
41		6	(a)	Leicester C	L	0-2		11,455
42		11	(h)	Ipswich T	L	1-2	Wallace	9,389

FINAL LEAGUE POSITION: 21st in Division One

Appearances

Sub Appeareances

Goals

Turner	Venison	Pickering	Bennett	Chisholm	Elliott	Berry	Gayle	West	Proctor	Walker	Hodgson	Corner	Wylde	Atkinson	Daniel	Cummins	Lemon	Cooke	Agboola	Wallace	Moore	Armstrong	Cornforth	
1	2	3	4	5	6	7	8	9	10	11														1
1	2	3	4	5	6	7	8	9	10*	11	12													2
1	2	3			6	12	8	9	10	11	4	5*	7											3
1	2	3	4		6	7		9		11			8	10	5									4
1	2	3	4	5	6	7	8	9		11					10									5
1	2	3	4	5	6		8	9	10	11			12		7*									6
1	2	3*	4	5	6		8	9	10	11			12		7									7
1	2		4	5	6	7	8		10	11			9		3									8
1	2	10	4	5	6*	7		9		11			8	12	3									9
1	2	3	4	5	6	10	8	12		11			9*		7									10
1	2	3	4*	5	6	10	8		9	11			12		7									11
1		3		5	6	4	7*	12	10		11		9	8	2									12
1	2	3	4		6		8*		10	11	7		9		5	12								13
1	2		5		6	4	8		10	11	7*		9		3	12								14
1	2	3	5	4*	6	8	12	9	10	11	7													15
1	2		4	5		6	8	9		11	7				3	10								16
1	2		4	5		6	8	9		11	7*				3	10	12							17
1	2		5	12	6	4	8	9*	10	11					3	7								18
1	2	3	5	7	6	4	8	9	10	11														19
1	2	3	4	5		6	8	9	10	11	7													20
1	2	3	4		6	8			10	11	7			12	5			9						21
1	2	3	5		6	4*			10	11	7			9	8	12								22
1	2	3	5			6	7	9	10*	11	8				4			12						23
1	2	3		5	6	12		9							10	11		7	4	8*				24
1		3	4		6	10		9			7	2*		12		11		8	5					25
1	2	3	4	5	6			9		11	7*				10				8	12				26
1	2	3	4	5	6	10*		12		11	9						7		8					27
1	2	3	4	5	6	10	12	9		11	7*								8					28
1	2	3	4	5	6	10*	12	9		11	7						8							29
1	2	3		5	6	10	12			11	9	4					8			7*				30
1	2	3	4	5						11	9				10	7			6*	8	12			31
1	2	3	4	5		12				11				7	10	6*				8	9			32
1	2	3	4	5	6	8				11					7*	10		12		9				33
1	2	3	4	5	6	10				11							7			8	9			34
1	2	3	4	5	6	10				11						12	7			8	9*			35
1	2	3	4	5	6	10				11						9	7			8				36
1	2	3	4	5		10				11	12					9	7		6*	8				37
1	2	3		5			12			11	9				6	10	7			8		4*		38
1	2	3	4	5	6*		12			11	9				7	10				8				39
1	2	3	4				7			11	9				5	10			6*	8		12		40
1	2	3	4	5		7				11*	9			12			10			8		6		41
1		3	4*		12	6					9			11			10	7		8		5	2	42
42	39	37	37	31	31	31	19	20	17	38	23	3	8	5	25	13	10	4	8	14	3	3	1	
				1	1	3	6	3			2		3	4		4	1	2		1	1	1		
	1	2	3	1		2	2	3	2	10	4		3	1						3	1			

1985-86

1	Aug	17	(h)	Blackburn R	L	0-2		21,202
2		20	(a)	Portsmouth	L	0-3		14,681
3		24	(a)	Crystal Pal	L	0-1		7,040
4		26	(h)	Oldham A	L	0-3		16,440
5		31	(a)	Millwall	L	0-1		7,910
6	Sep	7	(h)	Grimsby T	D	3-3	Swindlehurst 2, Gates (pen)	14,895
7		14	(a)	Leeds U	D	1-1	Gray	19,693
8		21	(a)	Shrewsbury T	W	2-1	Pickering 2	3,919
9		28	(h)	Huddersfield T	W	1-0	Gates	18,980
10	Oct	5	(a)	Charlton A	L	1-2	Gates	5,552
11		12	(h)	Hull C	D	1-1	Gray	16,613
12		19	(a)	Carlisle U	W	2-1	Elliott, Gayle	9,251
13		22	(h)	Middlesbrough	W	1-0	Gates	20,541
14		26	(h)	Norwich C	L	0-2		17,908
15	Nov	2	(a)	Fulham	W	2-1	Gates (pen), Bennett	5,795
16		9	(h)	Wimbledon	W	2-1	Swindlehurst 2	15,518
17		16	(a)	Barnsley	D	1-1	Swindlehurst	9,410
18		23	(h)	Brighton & HA	W	2-1	Gates, Bennett	14,712
19		30	(a)	Stoke C	L	0-1		9,034
20	Dec	7	(h)	Portsmouth	L	1-3	Gates	17,229
21		14	(a)	Blackburn R	L	0-2		6,045
22		22	(h)	Crystal Pal	D	1-1	Armstrong	16,710
23		26	(h)	Sheffield U	W	2-1	Gates, Bennett	17,643
24		28	(a)	Middlesbrough	L	0-2		19,774
25	Jan	1	(a)	Bradford C	L	0-2		8,369
26		11	(h)	Leeds U	W	4-2	Pickering 3 (1 pen), Wallace	15,139
27		18	(h)	Millwall	L	1-2	Gray	14,294
28	Feb	1	(a)	Oldham A	D	2-2	Proctor, Hodgson (pen)	3,827
29		8	(h)	Carlisle U	D	2-2	Kennedy 2	12,689
30	Mar	1	(a)	Huddersfield T	L	0-2		7,150
31		8	(h)	Charlton A	L	1-2	Proctor	11,885
32		15	(a)	Hull C	D	1-1	Wallace	9,295
33		22	(a)	Grimsby T	D	1-1	Armstrong	5,339
34		29	(h)	Bradford C	D	1-1	Ford	14,870
35		31	(a)	Sheffield U	L	0-1		9,839
36	Apr	5	(h)	Fulham	W	4-2	Elliott, Proctor 2, Wallace	11,338
37		9	(a)	Norwich C	D	0-0		17,752
38		12	(a)	Wimbledon	L	0-3		6,051
39		19	(h)	Barnsley	W	2-0	Futcher (og), Gayle	12,349
40		26	(a)	Brighton & HA	L	1-3	Proctor	9,189
41		29	(h)	Shrewsbury T	W	2-0	Gates, Proctor	15,507
42	May	3	(h)	Stoke C	W	2-0	Proctor (pen), Gray	20,631

FINAL LEAGUE POSITION: 18th in Division Two

Appearances

Sub Appearances

Goals

McDonagh	Venison	Gray	Agboola	Bennett	Elliott	Pickering	Wallace	Swindlehurst	Gates	Walker	Hodgson	Daniel	Chisholm	Berry	Gayle	Bolder	Burley	Kennedy	Atkinson	Corner	Proctor	Armstrong	Dibble	Lemon	Hetzke	Duncan	Ford	White	
1	2	3	4	5	6	7	8	9	10	11*	12																		1
1	2	3	4	5	6	7	8	9	10	11																			2
1	2	3	4*	5	6	7	8	9	10	11		12																	3
1	2	3		5	6*	7	12	9	10	11	8	4																	4
1	2	3			6	7		9	10	12	8	4	5	11*															5
1	2	3		5	6	7*		9	10	11	8	4			12														6
1	2	3		5	6	7		9	10	11	8	4																	7
	2	3	6	5		7		9	10	11	8*	4			12	1													8
	8	7		5	6			9	10	11		4				1	2	3											9
	8	7		5	6			9*	10	11	12	4				1	2	3											10
	8	7		5	6	12			10	11	9	4*				1	2	3											11
	8	7		5	6	4			10						9	1	2	3	11										12
	8	7		5	6	4	12		10						9	1	2	3	11*										13
	8	7		5	6	4*		9	10						11	1	2	3	12										14
	8	7		5	6	4		9	10						11	1	2	3											15
	4	7		5	6	8		9	10						11	1	2	3											16
	4	7		5	6	8*		9	10						11	1	2	3	12										17
	8	7		5		4		9	10						11	1	2	3		6									18
	4*	7		5	6	8		9	10	12					11	1	2	3											19
	8			5	6	4		9	10	11					7*	1	2	3	12										20
	8			5	6	4	7*	9	10	12						1	2	3		11									21
		4			6			9	10						12	1	2	3	7	5*	11	8							22
				5	6	4		9	10							1	2	3	7		11	8							23
				5	6	4	12		10						9	1	2	3	7*		11	8							24
			4	5*		12		9	10							1	2	3	7	6	11	8							25
	8				6	4		9	10							1	2	3	7	5	11								26
	8	12			6	4		9	10*							1	2	3	7	5	11								27
	8	4			6			9*	10	12					7	1	2	3		5	11								28
		4			6			9	10						8*	1	2	3	7	5	11	12							29
	8	12		5	6			9									2	3	7*		11	4			1	10			30
	8				6			9*	10						7		2	3			11	4	1	5	12				31
	8				6	12			10						7		2	3*			11	4	1	9	5				32
	11	8			6	12			10						7		2*	3				4		9	5	1			33
	8	11			6				10						7		2	3				4	1	9*	5			12	34
	11	8			6			9							12		2*	3				4	1	5			7	10	35
	10				6			9*							8			3			11	4	1	5			7	12	36
	2	4	6*					9	10						8			3			11		1	5			7	12	37
	2	10	6					9							12			3*			11	4	1	5			7	8	38
	2		6	5				9	10						8			3			11	4	1				7		39
	2	4		5	6			9	10						8			3			11		1				7		40
	2	4		5	6			9	10						8			3			11		1				7		41
	2	4		5	6			9	10	12					8*			3			11		1				7		42
7	36	32	12	28	32	22	14	25	38	10	9	8	1	1	20	22	27	32	10	9	19	13	12	4	8	1	8	2	
	2			2	5		1		2	6	1				3			3					1	1			1	2	
		4		3	2	5	3	5	9			1			2			2			7	2					1		

1986-87

#		Date		Venue	Opponent	Res	Score	Scorers	Att
1	Aug	23	(a)	Huddersfield T		W	2-0	Gray, Swindlehurst	9,937
2		30	(h)	Brighton & HA		D	1-1	Proctor (pen)	14,990
3	Sep	6	(a)	Blackburn R		L	1-6	Swindlehurst	7,115
4		13	(h)	Hull C		W	1-0	Gray	12,911
5		20	(a)	Ipswich T		D	1-1	Corner	12,824
6		27	(h)	Stoke C		W	2-0	Swindlehurst, Armstrong (pen)	14,394
7	Oct	1	(a)	Derby Co		L	2-3	Buchanan, Lemon	12,448
8		4	(h)	Portsmouth		D	0-0		16,938
9		11	(a)	Oldham A		D	1-1	Buchanan	7,088
10		18	(a)	Plymouth A		W	4-2	Buchanan 2, Armstrong, Lemon	13,482
11		21	(h)	Reading		D	1-1	Swindlehurst	17,114
12		25	(h)	Birmingham C		W	2-0	Gray, Buchanan	15,553
13	Nov	1	(a)	Sheffield U		L	1-2	Bennett	12,317
14		8	(h)	West Brom A		L	0-3		16,162
15		15	(a)	Grimsby T		D	1-1	Swindlehurst	7,065
16		22	(h)	Shrewsbury T		D	1-1	Armstrong	12,374
17		29	(a)	Crystal Palace		L	0-2		6,930
18	Dec	6	(h)	Millwall		D	1-1	Proctor	10,665
19		13	(a)	Barnsley		L	0-1		15,535
20		21	(h)	Blackburn R		W	3-0	Lemon, Gates, Buchanan	11,843
21		26	(a)	Leeds U		D	1-1	Gates	21,286
22		27	(h)	Grimsby T		L	0-1		13,769
23	Jan	24	(h)	Huddersfield T		W	2-1	Lemon, Buchanan	10,486
24		31	(a)	Reading		L	0-1		6,885
25	Feb	7	(a)	Brighton & HA		W	3-0	Gates, Curran, Bennett	7,820
26		14	(h)	Derby Co		L	1-2	Bennett	16,005
27		28	(h)	Ipswich T		W	1-0	Proctor (pen)	11,781
28	Mar	3	(a)	Hull C		L	0-1		5,713
29		14	(h)	Plymouth A		W	2-1	Buchanan, Lemon	10,062
30		17	(a)	Stoke C		L	0-3		9,420
31		21	(h)	Oldham A		L	0-2		10,250
32		28	(a)	Portsmouth		L	1-3	Gates	13,371
33		31	(a)	Birmingham C		L	0-2		5,563
34	Apr	4	(a)	West Brom A		D	2-2	Bertschin, Proctor (pen)	6,123
35		11	(h)	Sheffield U		L	1-2	Swindlehurst	8,544
36		18	(a)	Bradford C		L	2-3	Proctor 2 (1 pen)	11,483
37		20	(h)	Leeds U		D	1-1	Gates	14,725
38		25	(a)	Shrewsbury T		W	1-0	Bennett	5,431
39		28	(h)	Bradford C		L	2-3	Proctor 2 (1 pen)	16,545
40	May	2	(h)	Crystal Palace		W	1-0	Armstrong	11,461
41		5	(a)	Millwall		D	1-1	Armstrong	4,211
42		9	(h)	Barnsley		L	2-3	Bertschin, Gray	19,059

FINAL LEAGUE POSITION: 20th in Division Two

Appearances

Sub Appearances

Goals

44

Hesford	Burley	Gray	Armstrong	Hetzke	Bennett	Lemon	Proctor	Swindlehurst	Gates	Buchanan	Comer	Agboola	Kennedy	Atkinson	Doyle	Moore	Curran	Mimms	Saddington	Outterside	Bertschin	
1	2	3	4	5	6	7	8	9	10	11												1
1	2	3	4		6	7	8	9	10	11	5											2
1		3	4		6	7	8	9	10	11	5	2										3
1	2	10	4		6	7	8*	9		11	5		3	12								4
1	2	10*	4			7		9		11	5	6	3	12	8							5
1	2	10	4		6	7		9		11	5		3		8							6
1	2	10*	4		6	7		9	12	11	5		3		8							7
1	2	10	4		6	7		9	12	11	5		3*		8							8
1	2	10	4	5	6	7		9		11			3		8							9
1	2	10	4	5	6	7		9		11			3		8							10
1	2	10	4	5	6	7		9	12	11*			3		8							11
1	2	10	4	5	6	7		9	12	11			3		8*							12
1	2	10	4	5	6	7		9		11			3	8								13
1	2	3	4		6	7		9	10*	11	5				8	12						14
1	2	3	4	5	6	12	10	9		11*					8		7					15
1	2	3	4	5	6		10	9		11					8		7					16
1	2	3	4	5	6	12	10	9		11*					8		7					17
1	2		4	5	6		8	9		11			3		10		7					18
	2		4		6		10	9	12	11	5		3				7	1	8*			19
	2	11	4	5*	6	7	10	9	8	12			3					1				20
	2		4		6	7	8	9		11			3		10			1				21
	2		4		6	7	10		8	12	5		3		11	9*		1				22
1	2	3	4*		6	7	10	9	11	12					8				5			23
1	2	3	4	5	6	7	10	9*		11				12	8							24
1	2	3	4	5	6	9				11			10		8		7					25
1		3	4	5	6	9				11	12		10		8		7		2*			26
1	2	3	4		6	7*	12			11	5		10		8		9					27
1		3	4	5	6	11	10	9		12					8		7*					28
1	2	3	4	5	6	7	10	9		11					8							29
1		3	4	5	6	7	10	9		11		2*		12	8							30
1		3	4	5	6	7	10	9*		11				12	8					2		31
1	2*	3			6	7	10			11	12	5	4		8						9	32
1		3	12		6	2	10			11	4	5	7*		8						9	33
1		3	4	5	6	7	10	8		11					2						9	34
1		3	4	5	6	7	10	8		11*	12				2						9	35
1		5	4		6		10	8		11		2	3		7						9	36
1		5	7		6		10	8		11	4	2	3								9	37
1		5	7		6		10	8		11	4	2	3								9	38
1		5	7		6		10			11	4	2*	3		8	12					9	39
1		5	7	4	6		10	8		11			3		2						9	40
1		5	7	4	6		10	8		11*	12		3		2						9	41
1		5	7	4	6		10	8		11*	12		3		2						9	42
38	27	38	40	23	41	30	30	34	22	24	17	11	22	3	33	1	9	4	3	1	11	
		1			2	1			5	9			5		2							
		4	5		4	5	8	6	5	8	1						1				2	

45

1987-88

1	Aug	15	(a)	Brentford	W	1-0	Bertschin	7,559
2		22	(h)	Bristol R	D	1-1	Lemon	13,059
3		29	(a)	Doncaster R	W	2-0	Lemon, Owers	2,740
4		31	(h)	Mansfield T	W	4-1	Armstrong, Atkinson, MacPhail 2 (2 pens)	13,994
5	Sep	5	(a)	Walsall	D	2-2	Bertschin 2	6,909
6		12	(h)	Bury	D	1-1	Owers	13,227
7		15	(a)	Gillingham	D	0-0		9,184
8		19	(a)	Brighton & HA	L	1-3	MacPhail (pen)	8,949
9		26	(h)	Chester C	L	0-2		12,760
10		29	(a)	Fulham	W	2-0	Gabbiadini 2	6,996
11	Oct	3	(h)	Aldershot	W	3-1	MacPhail, Gabbiadini 2	12,542
12		10	(h)	Wigan A	W	4-1	Gates 2, Gabbiadini 2	13,974
13		17	(a)	Blackpool	W	2-0	MacPhail 2 (1 pen)	8,476
14		20	(a)	Bristol C	W	1-0	Owers	15,109
15		24	(h)	York C	W	4-2	Cornforth 2, Gabbiadini, Gates	19,314
16		31	(a)	Notts Co	L	1-2	MacPhail	8,854
17	Nov	3	(h)	Southend U	W	7-0	Gates 4, Atkinson 2, Gabbiadini	15,574
18		7	(h)	Grimsby T	D	1-1	Armstrong	18,197
19		21	(a)	Chesterfield	D	1-1	MacPhail (pen)	5,700
20		28	(h)	Port Vale	W	2-1	Gates, MacPhail (pen)	15,655
21	Dec	12	(a)	Northampton T	W	2-0	Lemon, Gabbiadini	7,279
22		20	(h)	Rotherham U	W	3-0	Gates 3	20,168
23		26	(a)	Chester C	W	2-1	MacPhail, Lemon	6,663
24		28	(h)	Preston NE	D	1-1	MacPhail (pen)	24,814
25	Jan	1	(h)	Doncaster R	W	3-1	Gabbiadini, Lemon 2	19,419
26		2	(a)	Bury	W	3-2	Valentine (og), Doyle, Gates	4,883
27		16	(h)	Brighton & HA	W	1-0	Lemon	17,404
28		30	(h)	Gillingham	W	2-1	Bennett, Gabbiadini	16,195
29	Feb	6	(h)	Walsall	D	1-1	Bennett	18,311
30		13	(a)	Preston NE	D	2-2	MacPhail, Gates	10,852
31		20	(h)	Brentford	W	2-0	Owers, Bertschin	15,458
32		24	(a)	Bristol R	L	0-1		4,501
33		27	(a)	Aldershot	L	2-3	MacPhail (pen), Gabbiadini	5,010
34	Mar	1	(h)	Fulham	W	2-0	Armstrong, Gabbiadini	11,379
35		5	(h)	Blackpool	D	2-2	Armstrong, Gates	15,513
36		12	(a)	Wigan A	D	2-2	Gabbiadini, Gates	6,949
37		19	(h)	Notts Co	D	1-1	Gabbiadini	24,071
38		26	(a)	York C	L	1-2	Pascoe	8,878
39	Apr	2	(a)	Grimsby T	W	1-0	Gabbiadini	7,001
40		4	(h)	Chesterfield	W	3-2	Lemon, Pascoe, Gabbiadini	21,886
41		9	(a)	Southend U	W	4-1	MacPhail (pen), Lemon, Gabbiadini, Pascoe	8,109
42		23	(h)	Bristol C	L	0-1		18,225
43		26	(a)	Mansfield T	W	4-0	Gates 2, Gabbiadini, Pascoe	6,930
44		30	(a)	Port Vale	W	1-0	Gates	7,569
45	May	2	(h)	Northampton T	W	3-1	MacPhail (pen), Armstrong, Gates	29,454
46		7	(a)	Rotherham U	W	4-1	Gabbiadini 2, MacPhail (pen), Bertschin	9,374

FINAL LEAGUE POSITION: 1st in Division Three

Appearances

Sub Appearances

Goals

No	Hardwick	Hay	Agboola	Bennett	MacPhail	Armstrong	Lemon	Proctor	Bertschin	Gates	Owers	Moore	Gray	Atkinson	Doyle	Buchanan	Hesford	Gabbiadini	Cornforth	Comer	Ord	Heathcote	McGuire	Pascoe	Carter	No
1	1	2	3	4	5	6	7	8	9	10*	11†	12	14													1
2	1	2	3	4	5	6	7	8	9	10*	11†	12	14													2
3	1	2	3	4	5	6	7	8	9*	10	11†	12	14													3
4	1	2	3	4	5	6	7	8	9	10				11												4
5	1	2	3	4	5	6	7†		9	10*	11	12	14		8											5
6	1	2	3	4	5	6	7†		9		11	12	14		8	10*										6
7		2	3	4	5	6	7		9	10	11				8		1									7
8		2	3	4	5	6†	7*		9	10	11		14	12	8		1									8
9		2	3*	4	5		7		9		6		12	11	8		1	10								9
10		2	3	4	5		7		9*		6	12	14	11†	8		1	10								10
11		2	3	4†	5		7*		9		6	12	14	11	8		1	10								11
12		2	3	4*	5				9		6	12	11		8		1	10	7							12
13		2	3		5		12		9*		6	14	11†		8		1	10	7	4						13
14		2	3		5		12		9		6	14	11†		8		1	10	7*	4						14
15		2	3		5				9		6	12	11*		8		1	10	7	4						15
16		2	3†		5	12	8		9		6	14	11				1	10	7*	4						16
17		2			5	8	12		9		6	3	11				1	10	7*			4†	14			17
18		2			5	7	12		14	9	6*	3	11	8			1	10†				4				18
19		2	3		5	7*	12		10	9	6		11	8			1					4				19
20		2	3	4	5		7		12	9	6		11	8			1	10*								20
21		2	3	4	5	11	7			9	6			8			1	10								21
22		2	3	4	5	11	7			9	6			8			1	10	8							22
23		2	3	4	5	11	7		12	9*	6			8			1	10								23
24		2	3	4	5	11	7		9*		6†	12	14	8			1	10								24
25		2	3	4	5	11†	7		12	9*			14	6	8		1	10								25
26		2	3	4	5	11	7		12	9	6			8			1	10*								26
27		2	3†	4	5	11	7		12	9	6*		14	8			1	10								27
28		2	3	4	5	11	7		12	9			6	8			1	10*								28
29		2	3	4	5	11	7			9			6	8			1	10								29
30		2	3	4	5	11	7†			9*			14	6	8		1	10	12							30
31		2	3	4	5	11			10	9	7		12	6*	8		1									31
32		2	3	4	5	11			10	9	7		14	6†	8*		1		12							32
33		2	3	4	5	11	12			9	7			6†			1	10	8*			14				33
34		2	3	4	5	11	8			9	7		6				1	10								34
35		2	3	4	5	11	8		14	9†	7		6*				1	10	12							35
36		2	3	4	5	11	8		12	9	7		6				1	10*								36
37		2	3	4	5		8			9	7	12		11	6		1	10*								37
38		2	3	4	5	11				9	7†		14		6		1	10				8*	12			38
39		2	3*	4	5	11	8†			9	7		14				1	10	12				6			39
40		2		4	5	11	7*			9	6		3				1	10			12		8			40
41		2		4	5	11	7			9	6		3				1	10*			12		8			41
42		2			5	11*	7		14	9†	6		3		12			10			4		8		1	42
43		2		4	5	11	7			9			3		6		1	10					8			43
44		2	12	4*	5	11	7			9			3		6		1	10					8			44
45		2		4	5	11	7			9			3		6		1	10					8			45
46		2		4	5	11	7*		14	9			3		6		1	10			12†		8			46
	6	46	37	38	46	36	35	4	14	42	37		12	21	31	1	39	35	8	4	4	1	8	1		
			1			1	6		11				9	22	1	1			4		4	1		1		
				2	16	5	9		5	19	4			3	1			21	2					4		

47

1988-89

1	Aug	27	(h)	Bournemouth	D	1-1	Bennett	17,998
2	Sep	3	(a)	Ipswich T	L	0-2		12,835
3		10	(h)	Bradford C	D	0-0		16,286
4		17	(a)	Birmingham C	L	2-3	Pascoe 2	6,871
5		20	(h)	Crystal Palace	D	1-1	Pascoe	13,150
6		24	(a)	Shrewsbury T	D	0-0		4,195
7	Oct	1	(h)	Oldham A	W	3-2	Gabbiadini, MacPhail (pen), Pascoe	12,529
8		4	(h)	Leeds U	W	2-1	Gabbiadini, Whitehurst	12,671
9		8	(a)	Walsall	L	0-2		6,150
10		15	(a)	Hull C	D	0-0		8,261
11		22	(h)	Swindon T	W	4-0	Owers, Gabbiadini 2, Whitehurst	13,520
12		25	(h)	Blackburn R	W	2-0	Gabbiadini, Hendry (og)	16,601
13		29	(a)	Manchester C	D	1-1	Armstrong	22,398
14	Nov	2	(a)	Oxford U	W	4-2	Whitehurst, Armstrong, Gabbiadini, MacPhail (pen)	6,270
15		5	(h)	Stoke C	D	1-1	Doyle	17,923
16		12	(a)	Chelsea	D	1-1	Gabbiadini	19,210
17		19	(h)	West Brom A	D	1-1	Bennett	18,141
18		26	(a)	Brighton & HA	L	0-3		10,039
19	Dec	3	(h)	Watford	D	1-1	MacPhail (pen)	16,330
20		10	(a)	Leicester C	L	1-3	Pascoe	11,093
21		18	(a)	Plymouth A	W	4-1	Armstrong, Pascoe, Gabbiadini, Gates	13,498
22		26	(h)	Barnsley	W	1-0	Dobbin (og)	21,994
23		31	(h)	Portsmouth	W	4-0	Gates, Ord, Armstrong, Pascoe	21,566
24	Jan	2	(a)	Bradford C	L	0-1		12,186
25		14	(h)	Oxford U	W	1-0	Owers	12,853
26		21	(a)	Bournemouth	W	1-0	Gates	8,992
27	Feb	4	(a)	Leeds U	L	0-2		31,984
28		11	(h)	Walsall	L	0-3		14,203
29		18	(a)	Swindon T	L	1-4	Armstrong	7,432
30		25	(h)	Hull C	W	2-0	Pascoe, Gabbiadini	14,719
31		28	(a)	Blackburn R	D	2-2	Gabbiadini 2 (1 pen)	8,288
32	Mar	11	(a)	Stoke C	L	0-2		12,489
33		14	(h)	Manchester C	L	2-4	Gabbiadini, Gates	16,101
34		18	(a)	Crystal Palace	L	0-1		9,108
35		21	(h)	Chelsea	L	1-2	Gabbiadini	14,714
36		25	(h)	Ipswich T	W	4-0	Gabbiadini 3 (1 pen), Owers	13,859
37		27	(a)	Barnsley	L	0-3		8,070
38	Apr	1	(h)	Birmingham C	D	2-2	Lemon, Gabbiadini	10,969
39		4	(h)	Plymouth A	W	2-1	Armstrong 2	9,003
40		8	(a)	Portsmouth	L	0-2		7,724
41		15	(a)	Oldham A	D	2-2	MacPhail, Hauser	5,944
42		22	(h)	Shrewsbury T	W	2-1	Hauser, Armstrong	9,427
43		29	(h)	Brighton & HA	W	1-0	Pascoe	12,856
44	May	1	(a)	Watford	W	1-0	Gabbiadini	13,499
45		6	(a)	West Brom A	D	0-0		10,451
46		13	(h)	Leicester C	D	2-2	Bennett, Pascoe	15,819

FINAL LEAGUE POSITION: 11th in Division Two

Appearances

Sub Appearances

Goals

Hesford	Kay	Agboola	Bennett	MacPhail	Doyle	Lemon	Armstrong	Gates	Gabbiadini	Pascoe	Owers	Ord	Gray	Cornforth	Whitehurst	Lynch	Ogilvie	Carter	Norman	Cullen	Barnes	Hauser	Hay	Atkinson	Williams	Wharton	Hawke	
1	2	3	4	5	6	7	8	9*	10	11	12																	1
1	2	3	4	5*	6	7†	8	9	10	11			12	14														2
1	2		4	5	6		8	9	10*	11	7		3	12														3
1	2		4	5	6		8*	9		11	7		3	12	10													4
1	2	3	4	5	6		8	9*	12	11	7†			14	10													5
1	2	3	4	5	6		8	9*		11	7		12		10													6
1		3		5	6		8	9		11	7	4	2		10													7
1		3		5	6		8	9		11	7	4	2		10													8
1		3		5	6		8	12	9	11	7	4	2		10*													9
1		3		5	6		8	12	9	11	7	4	2		10*													10
1		3	12	5	6		8	9		11	7	4	2*		10													11
1		3		5	6		8	9		11	7	4	2		10													12
1		3		5	6		8	9		11	7	4	2		10													13
1		3	12	5	6		8	9		11	7	4*	2		10													14
1		3*	12	5	6		8	9		11	7	4	2		10													15
1	7		4	5	6†		8	12	9*	11			2		10	3	14											16
1			4	5	6*		8	12	9	11	7		2		10	3												17
1		3	4	5	6*		8	12	9	11	7	14	2†		10													18
1		3	4	5	6		8	9		11	7		2		10													19
1		3	4†	5	6		8	12	9	11	7	14	2		10*													20
	2			5	6		8	9	10	11	7	4	3				1											21
	2			5	6		8	9	10	11	7	4	3				1											22
	2	14		5	6*		8	9	10	11	7	4	3†	12				1										23
	2			5	6	7	8	9	10	11		4	3					1										24
	2	12		5*		7	8	9		11	6	4	3		10			1										25
	2	12		5			8	9	10	11	7	4	3	6*				1										26
	2			5	6	12	8	9		11	7*	4	3		10			1										27
	2	7*		5	6		8	9		11		4	3		10			1		12								28
	2	12		5	6		8	9		11		4*	3		10			1	14	7†								29
	2	4		5	6		8	9*	10†	11			3	12				1	7	14								30
	2	4		5	6		8	9*	10	11			3					1	7	12								31
	2	4		5	6		8	9*	10	11		14	3					1	7†	12								32
	2	4		5	6*		8	9	10	11	7		3†					1		14	12							33
	2	4†		5	6	14	8	9*	10		7	11	3					1			12							34
	2			5		11	8		10		7	6	3			4		1			9							35
	2			5		14	8	12	10	11	7	6	3					1			9*		4†					36
	2			5	4†	14	8	12	10	11	7	6	3					1			9*							37
	2			5		4	8	9	10	11*	7	6	3					1		12†		14						38
	2			5		4	8	9	10		7	6	3					1						11*	12			39
	2	3		5	7	4*	8		10			6	12					1						11		9†	14	40
	2			5	7		8		10			6	3	4		11*		1			9			12				41
	2	3		5	7		8		10*	11		6		4				1			9					12		42
	2	3†		5	4		8	12		11	7	6	14		10			1			9*							43
	2	3		5		14	8	9	10*	11	7	6	4†					1								12		44
	2	3	4	5			8	9*	10	11	7	6						1								12		45
	2	3		5		14	8	12	10	11	7	4	6†	8*				1			9							46
20	11	25	37	45	35	12	45	27	35	39	36	31	36	10	17	4	2	24	3	11	6	1	2	1	1			
		4	3		6			10	1		2	3	4	5		1			4	7	1		1		3			
		3	4	1	1		8	4	18	10	3	1		3						2								

49

1989-90

1	Aug	19	(a)	Swindon T	W	2-0	Gates, Hawke	10,199
2		22	(h)	Ipswich T	L	2-4	Gates, Gabbiadini	15,965
3		27	(h)	Middlesbrough	W	2-1	Bennett, Pascoe	21,569
4	Sep	2	(a)	West Brom A	D	1-1	Gabbiadini	10,885
5		9	(h)	Watford	W	4-0	Armstrong, Gabbiadini 3	15,042
6		16	(a)	Blackburn R	D	1-1	MacPhail	10,329
7		24	(h)	Newcastle U	D	0-0		29,499
8		27	(a)	Leicester C	W	3-2	Armstrong, Hardyman (pen), Owers	10,843
9		30	(h)	Sheffield U	D	1-1	Deane (og)	22,760
10	Oct	7	(h)	Bournemouth	W	3-2	Gates 2, Gabbiadini	15,933
11		14	(a)	Leeds U	L	0-2		27,815
12		18	(a)	West Ham U	L	0-5		20,901
13		21	(h)	Bradford C	W	1-0	MacPhail	14,849
14		28	(a)	Stoke C	W	2-0	Bracewell, Gabbiadini	12,480
15		31	(h)	Barnsley	W	4-2	Gates 2, Hardyman (pen), Bennett	14,234
16	Nov	4	(a)	Oldham A	L	1-2	Owers	8,829
17		11	(h)	Wolverhampton W	D	1-1	Hardyman (pen)	20,660
18		18	(h)	Plymouth A	W	3-1	Gabbiadini, Owers, Ord	15,033
19		25	(a)	Brighton & HA	W	2-1	Gabbiadini, Owers	8,681
20	Dec	2	(h)	Swindon T	D	2-2	Armstrong, Hauser	15,849
21		9	(a)	Ipswich T	D	1-1	Owers	13,833
22		16	(a)	Portsmouth	D	3-3	Bennett, Hardyman, Gabbiadini	7,127
23		26	(h)	Oxford U	W	1-0	Gabbiadini	24,075
24		30	(h)	Port Vale	D	2-2	Gabbiadini, Hauser	21,354
25	Jan	1	(a)	Hull C	L	2-3	Hauser, Owers	9,346
26		14	(a)	Middlesbrough	L	0-3		17,698
27		20	(h)	West Brom A	D	1-1	Gabbiadini	15,583
28	Feb	4	(a)	Newcastle U	D	1-1	Gabbiadini	31,572
29		10	(h)	Blackburn R	L	0-1		16,043
30		17	(a)	Watford	D	1-1	Hauser	9,093
31		24	(h)	Brighton & HA	W	2-1	Hauser 2	14,528
32	Mar	3	(a)	Plymouth A	L	0-3		7,299
33		10	(h)	Leicester C	D	2-2	Gabbiadini, Armstrong	13,017
34		17	(a)	Bournemouth	W	1-0	Gabbiadini	6,328
35		20	(h)	Leeds U	L	0-1		17,851
36		24	(h)	West Ham U	W	4-3	Brady, Hardyman (pen), Owers, Gabbiadini	13,896
37		31	(a)	Bradford C	W	1-0	Brady	9,826
38	Apr	3	(a)	Sheffield U	W	3-1	Bracewell, Gabbiadini 2	20,588
39		7	(h)	Stoke C	W	2-1	Gabbiadini, Armstrong	17,119
40		10	(a)	Barnsley	L	0-1		11,141
41		14	(h)	Hull C	L	0-1		17,437
42		16	(a)	Oxford U	W	1-0	Gabbiadini	6,053
43		21	(h)	Portsmouth	D	2-2	Armstrong 2	14,379
44		28	(a)	Wolverhampton W	W	1-0	Hardyman	19,463
45	May	1	(a)	Port Vale	W	2-1	Owers, Hardyman	9,447
46		5	(h)	Oldham A	L	2-3	Owers, Armstrong	22,243

FINAL LEAGUE POSITION: 6th in Division Two

Appearances

Sub Appearances

Goals

Football appearances / results grid.

Norman	Agboola	Hardyman	Bennett	MacPhail	Owers	Cullen	Armstrong	Gates	Gabbiadini M	Pascoe	Comforth	Hawke	Ord	Bracewell	Carter	Hauser	Kay	Gabbiadini R	Atkinson	Heathcote	Brady	Williams	#
1	2	3	4*	5	6	7†	8	9	10	11	12	14											1
1	2	3		5	6	7	8	9	10	11			4										2
1	2	3	4	5	6		8	9	10	11				7									3
1	2	3	4	5	6		8	9*	10	11		12		7									4
	2	3	4	5	6	12	8	9	10	11*				7	1								5
	2	3	4	5	6*	12	8	9†	10	11				7	1	14							6
	2	3	4	5	6		8	9	10	11				7	1								7
	2	3	4	5	6		8	9	10	11				7	1								8
	2*	3	4	5	6	12	8	9†	10	11				7	1	14							9
		3	4	5	6		8	9	10	11				7	1		2						10
	2	3	4	5	6	12	8	9*	10†	11				7	1				14				11
		3	4	5	6	12	8	9†	10	11*				7	1	14	2						12
		3	4	5	6		8	9	10	11				7	1		2						13
		3*	4	5	6	12	8	9	10	11				7	1		2						14
		3	4	5†	6	12	8	9	10	11			14	7*	1		2						15
	2	3†	4		6	12	8	9*	10	11			5	7	1	14							16
		3	4		6		8	9	10	11			5	7	1		2						17
	2	3*	4		6		8	9	10	11			5	7	1	12							18
		3	4		6		8	9	10	11			5	7*	1	12	2						19
	2	3	4		6		8	9	10	11†			5*	7	1	14	12						20
	2	3	4		6		8	9	10	11			5	7	1								21
1	2	3	4	7	6		8	9*	10	11					5				12				22
1	2	3	4		6		8	9*	10	11	7				5				12				23
1	2	3	4		6		8	9*	10	11				14	5				12		7†		24
1	14	3†	4	5	6		8	9*	10	11				7			2		12				25
1	3*	9	4	5	6		8		10	11				7			2		12				26
12	3	4	5*	6	11†		8		10			14		7	1		9		2				27
1	4	3		5	6	12	8*	9	10					7			2		11				28
1	4	3		5			8	9*	10	11				7			2		12	6			29
1	4	3		5		11*	8		10			12		7			2	9		6			30
1		3	4	5		11	8		10					7			2	9		6			31
1	12	3*	4	5	11		8		10			14		7			2	9†		6			32
1	3		4	5	6		8		10		12			7			2	9			11*		33
1	3		4	5	6		8		10	12				7			2	9†	14		11*		34
1	3		4	5	6		8	9*	10	11				7			2		12				35
1	12	3*		5	6		8		10	11				7			2			4	9		36
1	12	3	4*	5	6		8		10	9				7			2				11		37
1		3		5	6		8		10	11				7			2			4	9		38
1		3		5	6		8	12	10	9				7			2			4	11*		39
1		3		5	6		8	12	10	9				7			2			4	11*		40
1	12	3	4	5	6	14	8	9	10					7†			2				11*		41
1	11	3	4†	5	6	14	8	9	10		12						2		7*				42
1	11	3		5	6		8	9	10					7			2			4			43
1	11	3	4	5	6		8	9	10					7			2						44
1	11	3	4*	5	6		8	9	10					7			2				12		45
1	11†	3		5	6		8	9*	10					7	12		2		14	4			46
28	30	42	36	38	43	5	46	34	46	32	1	1	6	36	18	6	31		11	6	9	1	
	6				11			2			1	1	7	1	1	12	1	1	2	2	2		
		7	3	2	9		8	6	21	1		1	1	2		6							

51

1990-91

1	Aug	25	(a)	Norwich C	L	2-3	Davenport, Gabbiadini	17,247
2		28	(h)	Tottenham H	D	0-0		30,214
3	Sep	1	(h)	Manchester U	W	2-1	Owers, Bennett	26,105
4		8	(a)	Chelsea	L	2-3	Gabbiadini, Brady	19,424
5		15	(h)	Everton	D	2-2	Davenport (pen), Gabbiadini	25,004
6		22	(a)	Wimbledon	D	2-2	Armstrong, Davenport	6,143
7		29	(h)	Liverpool	L	0-1		31,107
8	Oct	6	(a)	Aston Villa	L	0-3		26,017
9		20	(h)	Luton T	W	2-0	Gabbiadini, Davenport	20,025
10		27	(a)	Arsenal	L	0-1		38,539
11	Nov	3	(h)	Manchester C	D	1-1	Davenport	23,137
12		10	(h)	Coventry C	D	0-0		20,101
13		17	(a)	Nottingham F	L	0-2		22,757
14		24	(a)	Sheffield U	W	2-0	Gabbiadini 2	19,179
15	Dec	1	(h)	Derby Co	L	1-2	Armstrong	21,212
16		8	(a)	Tottenham H	D	3-3	Pascoe 2, Davenport	30,431
17		15	(h)	Norwich C	L	1-2	Armstrong	18,693
18		23	(h)	Leeds U	L	0-1		23,773
19		26	(a)	Crystal Palace	L	1-2	Rush	15,560
20		29	(a)	QPR	L	2-3	Pascoe, Ball (pen)	11,072
21	Jan	1	(h)	Southampton	W	1-0	Ball (pen)	19,757
22		12	(a)	Manchester U	L	0-3		45,934
23		19	(h)	Chelsea	W	1-0	Pascoe	20,038
24	Feb	2	(a)	Everton	L	0-2		23,124
25		16	(h)	Nottingham F	W	1-0	Gabbiadini	20,394
26		23	(a)	Coventry C	D	0-0		10,453
27	Mar	2	(a)	Derby Co	D	3-3	Armstrong, Gabbiadini, Ball	16,027
28		9	(h)	Sheffield U	L	0-1		23,238
29		16	(a)	Liverpool	L	1-2	Armstrong	37,582
30		23	(h)	Aston Villa	L	1-3	Davenport	21,099
31		30	(h)	Crystal Palace	W	2-1	Brady, Rush	19,704
32	Apr	2	(a)	Leeds U	L	0-5		28,132
33		6	(h)	QPR	L	0-1		17,899
34		13	(a)	Southampton	L	1-3	Hauser	16,812
35		20	(a)	Luton T	W	2-1	Armstrong, Pascoe	11,157
36		23	(h)	Wimbledon	D	0-0		24,036
37	May	4	(h)	Arsenal	D	0-0		22,606
38		11	(a)	Manchester C	L	2-3	Gabbiadini, Bennett	39,194

FINAL LEAGUE POSITION: 19th in Division One

Appearances

Sub Appearances

Goals

Norman	Kay	Agboola	Bennett	MacPhail	Owers	Bracewell	Armstrong	Davenport	Gabbiadini	Atkinson	Cullen	Hauser	Ball	Hardyman	Brady	Ord	Smith	Carter	Pascoe	Hawke	Rush	Williams	Mooney	Cornforth	
1	2	3	4	5	6	7	8	9	10†	11*	12	14													1
1	2	3	4		6	7	8	9	10		12		5	11*											2
1	2	3	4		6	7*	8	9	10†			14	5	11	12										3
1	2	3	4		6		8	9	10	7			5	11*	12										4
1	2	3*	4		6	7	8	9	10				5	11	12										5
1	2		4		6	7	8	9	10*		12		5	11		3									6
1	2		4		6	7	8	9	10	11*	12		5			3									7
1	2		4		6	7	8	9	10		11		5				3								8
1	2		4		6	7	8	9	10				5	11			3								9
1	2		4		6	7	8	9	10		12		5	11					3*						10
1	2		4		6	7	8	9	10	11*			5	3	12										11
	2		4		6	7	8	9	10				5	3				1	11						12
1	2		4		6	7	8	9	10*				5	3					11	12					13
1	2		4		6	7	8	9	10				5	3					11						14
1	2		4		6	7	8	9	10				5	3					11						15
1	2		4		6	7	8	9	10				5	3					11						16
1	2				6	7	8	9	10				5	3			4		11						17
1	2		4		6	7	8		10				5	3			9		11*	12					18
1	2		4		6	7	8		10*				5	3			9		11		12				19
1	2		4		6	7	8	9*					5	14		3			11	12†	10				20
1	2		4		6	7	8						5	3					11	9	10				21
1			4		6	7	8		10				5	14		3			11	12	9*	2†			22
1			4		6	7	8	9	10*	2			5	3					11	12					23
1			4		6	7	8	9	10	12			5	3			2		11*						24
1			4		2	7	8	9	10				5	3					11		6				25
1			4		2	7	8	9	10				5	3					11		6				26
1			4		2	7	8	9	10				5	3*		12			11		6				27
1			4		2	7	8	9	10				5		12	3			11		6*				28
1	6†		4		2	7	8		10*				5	3		12			11	9			14		29
1	14		4		2	7	8*	12					5	3			10		11	9			6†		30
1	6		4		2	7	8						5	3			10		11	9					31
1	6		4		2	7	8*	12					5	3			10		11†	9			14		32
1	14		4		2	7	8	9					5	3*			10†		11	12	6				33
1	11		4		2	7	8				9		5	3						10*	6				34
1	11†		4		2	7	8	12			9		5	3		14					6		10*		35
1			4		2	7	8	9	10†	11*			5	3	14	12					6				36
1	11		4		2	7		9	10				5	3		12					6		8*		37
1	11		4		2	7		9	10			14	5	3*		12					6		8†		38
37	28	5	37	1	38	37	35	27	30	4	2	5	33	30	4	12	9	1	25	3	8	1	5	1	
	2								2	1	2	3	5		2	10	2			4	3		1	1	
			2	1		6	7	9					1	3		2			5	2					

1991-92

#						Result		Scorers	Attendance
1	Aug	17	(h)	Derby Co	D	1-1		Armstrong	20,509
2		20	(a)	Barnsley	W	3-0		Owers, Armstrong, Pascoe	12,454
3		24	(a)	Millwall	L	1-4		Owers (pen)	10,016
4		31	(h)	Oxford U	W	2-0		Gabbiadini, Armstrong	16,151
5	Sep	3	(a)	Portsmouth	L	0-1			9,621
6		7	(h)	Blackburn R	D	1-1		Atkinson	17,043
7		14	(a)	Swindon T	L	3-5		Owers, Gabbiadini, Armstrong	11,417
8		17	(a)	Charlton A	W	4-1		Owers (pen), Gabbiadini 3	5,807
9		21	(h)	Grimsby T	L	1-2		Pascoe	16,535
10		28	(a)	Middlesbrough	L	1-2		Brady	19,424
11	Oct	5	(h)	Brighton & HA	W	4-2		Beagrie, Rush 2, Armstrong	15,119
12		12	(a)	Cambridge U	L	0-3			7,857
13		19	(a)	Port Vale	D	3-3		Brady 2, Ball	7,525
14		26	(h)	Bristol R	D	1-1		Bennett	14,746
15	Nov	2	(h)	Watford	W	3-1		Byrne 2, Armstrong	12,790
16		5	(a)	Ipswich T	W	1-0		Armstrong	9,768
17		9	(a)	Bristol C	L	0-1			10,570
18		17	(h)	Newcastle U	D	1-1		Davenport	29,224
19		23	(a)	Plymouth A	L	0-1			6,007
20		30	(h)	Southend U	L	1-2		Byrne	13,575
21	Dec	7	(a)	Wolverhampton W	L	0-1			11,922
22		14	(h)	Leicester C	W	1-0		Goodman	15,094
23		21	(h)	Portsmouth	W	1-0		Awford (og)	14,432
24		26	(a)	Tranmere R	L	0-1			13,658
25		28	(a)	Oxford U	L	0-3			6,140
26	Jan	1	(h)	Barnsley	W	2-0		Armstrong, Goodman	16,107
27		11	(a)	Millwall	W	6-2		Hardyman, Byrne, Goodman 3, Davenport	16,533
28		18	(a)	Derby Co	W	2-1		Goodman, Byrne	15,384
29	Feb	1	(h)	Port Vale	D	1-1		Armstrong	19,488
30		8	(a)	Bristol R	L	1-2		Byrne	6,318
31		11	(h)	Tranmere R	D	1-1		Hardyman	18,060
32		22	(a)	Southend U	L	0-2			7,473
33		29	(h)	Wolverhampton W	W	1-0		Byrne (pen)	20,106
34	Mar	14	(a)	Watford	L	0-1			8,091
35		21	(h)	Bristol C	L	1-3		Atkinson	18,933
36		29	(a)	Newcastle U	L	0-1			30,306
37	Apr	8	(a)	Leicester C	L	2-3		Bennett, Goodman	16,533
38		11	(h)	Charlton A	L	1-2		Bennett	21,326
39		14	(h)	Ipswich T	W	3-0		Goodman 2, Rush	22,131
40		16	(h)	Plymouth A	L	0-1			28,813
41		18	(a)	Grimsby T	L	0-2			8,864
42		20	(h)	Middlesbrough	W	1-0		Davenport	25,093
43		25	(a)	Brighton & HA	D	2-2		Goodman, Rogan	9,851
44		27	(h)	Swindon T	D	0-0			16,917
45		29	(a)	Blackburn R	D	2-2		Armstrong, Davenport	15,079
46	May	2	(h)	Cambridge U	D	2-2		Goodman, Rush	19,042

FINAL LEAGUE POSITION: 18th in Division Two

Appearances

Sub Appearances

Goals

Norman	Williams	Hardyman	Bennett	Ord	Owers	Bracewell	Atkinson	Armstrong	Gabbiadini	Pascoe	Hauser	Sampson	Kay	Ball	Davenport	Agboola	Rush	Beagrie	Brady	Rogan	Cullen	Byrne	Russell	Goodman	Mooney	Carter	Hawke	Gray	Smith	
1	2	3	4	5	6	7	8	9	10	11																				1
1	2	3	4	5	6	7	8	9	10	12	11*																			2
1	2	3	4	5†	6	7	8*	9	10	12	11	14																		3
1		3	4		6	7	8	9	10		11*		2	5	12															4
1		3	4		6	7	8	9	10	12	11*		2	5																5
1			4		6	7	8*	9	10	12	11		2	5		3														6
1		3	4		6	7	8†	9	10*	11	14		2	5	12															7
1		3	4		6	7		9	10	11			2	5	8															8
1		3	4		6	7		9	10*	11	12		2	5	8															9
1		3	4		7	6*		9					2	5	8		10	11	12											10
1					6	7		9				4	2	5	8		10	11		3										11
1		10†			6	7		9				4	2	5	14			11	12	3	8*									12
1			4		6	7		9					2	5	10*		12	11	8	3										13
1			4†		7	6		9		12		14	2	5				11	8*	3		10								14
1			4			7	12	9		11			2	5	6*		8†			3		10	14							15
1			4			7		9		11			2	5	6		8			3		10								16
1			4		12	7†		9		11			2	5	6		8*			3		10	14							17
1			4		12	7		9		11	14		2	5	6*		8†			3		10								18
1			4		12	7		9		11*			2	5	6		8			3		10†	14							19
1			4		11	7		9		12		14	2	5	6†					3		10		8*						20
1	14		4		11	7		9					2	5	6†		12			3		10		8*						21
1			4		6	7		9		12			2	5			11*			3		10		8						22
1		11	4		6	7		9		12			2	5			10*			3				8						23
1	9†	10*	4		6	7				14	12		2	5			11			3				8						24
1	14		4		6*	7		9					2	5	12		11			3†		10		8						25
1		3	4		6	7		9					2	5								10		8						26
1		5	4		6*	7	11	9					2		12					3		10		8						27
1		5	4			7	11†	9					2	14	6*		12			3		10		8						28
1		5	4			7	11	9†					2	14	6*		12			3		10		8						29
1		5	4			7*	11	9				14	2		12		6†			3		10		8						30
1		5	4				11	9		7			2		6					3		10		8						31
1	12	5				7	11	9				4	2		6*					3		10		8						32
1		5				7	11	9				4	2	12	6*				14	3		10		8†						33
1	14	5				7	11†	9				4	2		8*		6			3		10		12						34
1				5*		7	11	9				4	2		8		6†			3		10		12	14					35
		5				7	11	9				4	2		8*		6			3		10		12		1				36
1		5	4				11	9					2		8		6*			3		10			7	12				37
1		5	4				11	9					2		8*		6			3		10		12	7					38
1		5	4		14		11	9					2		12		6			3		10		8*			7†			39
1		5†	4		14		11	9					2		12		6			3		10*		8			7			40
1		5	4		14	7	11	9					2		12		6*			3		10		8†						41
1	12	3	4			7	11	9*			6		2	8			14							5					10†	42
1	12		4		6	7	11*	9†					2	5						3		10	14	8						43
1		5	12		6	7	11					4*	2		9†					3		10		8				14		44
1		5	4					9		11	6*		2									10		8		7†	14	12	3	45
		3			6			9		11			2	5			9		7			10		8			1			46
44	4	29	38	5	24	39	29	40	9	12	5	7	41	31	25	1	20	5	4	33	1	27	1	20	6	2	2	2	2	
	3	3	1	1	6	1				8	7	1		2	11		5		4			3	2	3			2	1		
		2	3		4		2	10	5	2		1		4	4		1			3		1		7	11					

1992-93

#	Month	Date		Opponent	Res	Score	Scorers	Attendance
1	Aug	15	(a)	Swindon T	L	0-1		11,094
2		22	(h)	Tranmere R	W	1-0	Cunnington	16,667
3		29	(a)	Bristol C	D	0-0		14,076
4	Sep	5	(h)	Charlton A	L	0-3		17,954
5		12	(a)	Oxford U	W	1-0	Rush	6,003
6		19	(a)	Cambridge U	L	1-2	Rush	5,383
7		26	(h)	Bristol R	D	1-1	Byrne	15,593
8		29	(a)	Watford	L	1-2	Goodman	6,263
9	Oct	3	(h)	Millwall	W	2-0	Goodman 2	14,871
10		11	(a)	West Ham U	L	0-6		10,326
11		18	(h)	Newcastle U	L	1-2	Armstrong	28,098
12		24	(a)	Portsmouth	L	0-2		10,689
13		31	(h)	Notts Co	D	2-2	Owers, Ball	15,473
14	Nov	3	(h)	Wolverhampton W	W	2-0	Cunnington, Goodman	15,144
15		7	(a)	Peterborough U	L	2-5	Davenport (pen), Rush	8,193
16		15	(h)	Leicester C	L	1-2	Davenport	14,945
17		21	(a)	Derby Co	W	1-0	Goodman	17,581
18		28	(a)	Southend U	W	1-0	Sampson	4,584
19	Dec	5	(h)	Barnsley	W	2-1	Gray Mic, Cunnington	17,395
20		12	(h)	Brentford	L	1-3	Cunnington	16,972
21		19	(a)	Luton T	D	0-0		8,286
22		28	(h)	Grimsby T	W	2-0	Goodman, Rush	20,771
23	Jan	9	(h)	Cambridge U	D	3-3	Mooney, Rush, Atkinson	16,778
24		16	(a)	Bristol R	D	2-2	Rush, Cunnington	6,140
25		27	(h)	Watford	L	1-2	Ball	14,703
26	Feb	6	(h)	Swindon T	L	0-1		17,234
27		9	(h)	Oxford U	W	2-0	Goodman (pen), Gray Mic	13,314
28		13	(a)	Charlton A	W	1-0	Goodman (pen)	8,151
29		20	(h)	Bristol C	D	0-0		17,122
30		27	(h)	West Ham U	D	0-0		19,068
31	Mar	6	(a)	Millwall	D	0-0		8,761
32		10	(a)	Leicester C	L	2-3	Goodman, Armstrong	15,609
33		13	(h)	Peterborough U	W	3-0	Davenport, Goodman, Cunnington	18,372
34		16	(a)	Birmingham C	L	0-1		10,934
35		21	(a)	Barnsley	L	0-2		7,278
36		24	(h)	Derby Co	W	1-0	Cunnington	17,246
37		27	(a)	Wolverhampton W	L	1-2	Harford	12,731
38	Apr	3	(h)	Southend U	L	2-4	Harford, Goodman	15,071
39		6	(a)	Brentford	D	1-1	Goodman	9,302
40		10	(h)	Birmingham C	L	1-2	Davenport	16,382
41		12	(a)	Grimsby T	L	0-1		8,090
42		17	(h)	Luton T	D	2-2	Goodman 2	16,493
43		25	(a)	Newcastle U	L	0-1		30,364
44	May	1	(h)	Portsmouth	W	4-1	Goodman 2 (2 pen), Gray Mar, Armstrong	21,309
45		4	(a)	Tranmere R	L	1-2	Atkinson	9,685
46		8	(a)	Notts Co	L	1-3	Ball	14,417

FINAL LEAGUE POSITION: 21st in Division One

Appearances

Sub Appearances

Goals

Norman	Ball	Bennett	Butcher	Smith	Owers	Cunnington	Goodman	Colquhoun	Byrne	Atkinson	Davenport	Armstrong	Carter	Kay	Ord	Rogan	Rush	Gray Martin	Gray Michael	Sampson	Mooney	Hawke	Harford	Howey	
1	2	3	4	5	6†	7	8	9*	10	11	12	14													1
	6		5	3	4	7	8*	9†	10		12	14	1	2	11										2
	6	9	5		4	7	8		10		12		1	2	11	3*									3
	6	9	5		4	7	8	14	10†		12		1	2	11*	3									4
	6	9	5		4*	7	8	12					1	2		3	10								5
	6	9*	5		4†	7	8			12	14	11	1			3	10	2							6
	6		5		4	7	8		10	12		11*	1			3	9	2							7
	6			5	4	7	8		10*	9†	12	11	1		14	3		2							8
	6	5			4	7	8			12	9	11	1	2		3		10*							9
	6	5			4	7*	8			12	9	11†	1	2		3		14	10						10
	6	5			4	7	8			10	9	12	1	2		3		11*							11
	6				4	7†	8	14		10	9*	11	1	2	5	3	12								12
1	6				4	7	8			10	9	11		2	5	3									13
	6				4	7	8			10	9	11		2	5	3									14
	6	12			4	7†	8			10	9	11		2	5	3*	14								15
1	6	12	5		4†	7	8			10	9	11		2*		3	14								16
1	6*		5		4	7	8			10	9†	11		2		3	14		12						17
1			5		4†	7		14		10	9	11		2		3*	8		12	6					18
1	6		5			7	8*	12		10	9†	11		2					3	4	14				19
1	6		5			7				10		11		2			9		3	4	8*	12			20
1	6		5			7					9†	11		2	4		10		3		8	14			21
1	6		5			7	8				12	11		2	4		10*		3		9				22
1	6		5			7	8			14		11		2	4		10		3†		9				23
1	6		5			7	8			3	12	11		2	4†		10	14			9*				24
1	6		5			7		12		4	8	11		2			10*		3		9				25
1	6		5	3			8			4	9*	11		2			10			7					26
1	6		5	3			8			4	9	11		2		7*	10		12						27
1	6		5	3			8			4*	9	11		2	12		10			7					28
1	6		5	3*			8			4	9	11		2	12		10	14		7†					29
1	6		5				8	14		4	9	11		2			10		3	7†					30
1	6		5		7		8			4	9	11		2					3	14	10†				31
1	6		5		7		8			4	9	11		2			10		3						32
1	6		5		7*		8	12		4	9	11		2					3						33
1	6		5		10	7	8			4	9	11		2					3						34
1	6	2	5		4	7	8	10*			12	11			3†					14			9		35
1	6	2†	5		4	7	8				10	11							3	14			9		36
1	6		5		4	7	8				10	11		2					3				9		37
1	6		5		4	7	8				10	11		2					3				9		38
1	6		5		4	7	8			10		11		2					3				9		39
1		6*	5		4	7	8			10	12	11		2					3				9		40
1	6†		5		4	7	8			10		11		2	14				3				9		41
1	6		5		4	7	8			10	12	11		2					3				9*		42
1			5			7	8	4*		10	12	11		2†				14	3				9		43
1		6*	5		4	7†	8	12		10	9	11						2	3					14	44
1	6		5		4	7	8			10	9	11						2*	3				12		45
1	6	2*	5		4†	7	8			10	14	11						12	3				9		46
33	43	14	37	7	33	38	41	12	6	31	20	41	13	36	21	12	12	9	23	4	10	-	10	-	
		1	1		1		8			5	13	4			3	1	6	3	4	1	2	2	1	1	
		3			1	7	16		1	2	4	3					6		1	2	1	1	2		

1993-94

1	Aug	14	(a)	Derby Co	L	0-5		18,027
2		21	(h)	Charlton A	W	4-0	Goodman, Gray Michael, Cunnington, Armstrong	17,647
3		28	(a)	Notts Co	L	0-1		9,166
4	Sep	12	(a)	Crystal Palace	L	0-1		11,318
5		18	(h)	Wolves	L	0-2		18,292
6		25	(a)	Watford	D	1-1	Owers	7,694
7		28	(h)	Grimsby T	D	2-2	Goodman, Ord	15,488
8	Oct	2	(h)	Peterborough U	W	2-0	Gray P, Owers	17,846
9		9	(h)	Birmingham C	W	1-0	Howey	19,264
10		17	(a)	Middlesbrough	L	1-4	Goodman	12,772
11		20	(h)	Luton T	W	2-0	Goodman, Smith M	13,760
12		23	(h)	West Brom A	W	1-0	Ord	19,505
13		30	(a)	Bristol C	L	0-2		8,162
14	Nov	3	(a)	Stoke C	L	0-1		13,551
15		6	(h)	Portsmouth	L	1-2	Smith M	17,146
16		13	(a)	Tranmere R	L	1-4	Goodman	8,497
17		20	(h)	Southend U	L	0-2		15,425
18		27	(h)	Nottingham F	L	2-3	Gray P, Smith M	16,968
19	Dec	4	(a)	Portsmouth	W	1-0	Smith M	11,891
20		18	(h)	Derby Co	W	1-0	Gray P	16,001
21		27	(a)	Bolton W	D	0-0		18,496
22		28	(h)	Millwall	W	2-1	Gray P, Russell	19,283
23	Jan	1	(a)	Leicester C	L	1-2	Gray P (pen)	19,615
24		3	(h)	Barnsley	W	1-0	Gray P	19,302
25		11	(a)	Oxford U	W	3-0	Smith M 2, Goodman	5,877
26		16	(h)	Middlesbrough	W	2-1	Gray P (pen), Howey	16,473
27		22	(a)	Birmingham C	D	0-0		15,884
28	Feb	5	(a)	West Brom A	L	1-2	Goodman	17,089
29		12	(h)	Bristol C	D	0-0		16,816
30		22	(a)	Charlton A	D	0-0		7,904
31		25	(a)	Luton T	L	1-2	Howey	9,367
32	Mar	5	(h)	Notts Co	W	2-0	Russell, Gray P	16,269
33		16	(h)	Crystal Palace	W	1-0	Gray P	15,892
34		19	(h)	Watford	W	2-0	Russell 2	16,479
35		26	(a)	Peterborough U	W	3-1	Russell, Gray P 2	8,753
36		29	(a)	Barnsley	L	0-4		10,042
37	Apr	2	(h)	Bolton W	W	2-0	Russell 2	18,574
38		6	(a)	Millwall	L	1-2	Melville	10,244
39		9	(h)	Leicester C	L	2-3	Goodman, Melville	17,198
40		12	(a)	Grimsby T	W	1-0	Smith M	4,732
41		19	(h)	Stoke C	L	0-1		17,406
42		23	(a)	Southend U	W	1-0	Smith M	4,734
43		26	(h)	Oxford U	L	2-3	Gray P (pen), Armstrong	14,712
44		30	(h)	Tranmere R	W	3-2	Gray P 2, Russell	15,167
45	May	3	(a)	Wolves	D	1-1	Goodman	25,079
46		8	(a)	Nottingham F	D	2-2	Goodman, Russell	27,010

FINAL LEAGUE POSITION: 12th in Division One

Appearances

Sub. Appearances

Goals

Chamberlain	Kay	Gray Mi.	Ferguson	Melville	Sampson	Owers	Goodman	Howey	Cunnington	Armstrong	Atkinson	Power	Smith M	Gray Ma.	Bennett	Russell	Gray P	Brodie	Ord	Ball	Rush	Lawrence	Rodgerson	Kubicki	Norman	Smith A	No.
1	2	3	4*	5	6	7	8	9†	10	11	12	14															1
1	2	5		6		7	8	12	9	11			10*	14	4											3†	2
1			6		2	7†	8		9	11	5			3	4	10*	12	14									3
1			5*	6		2	8			11	12	14		7	4	9	10†		3								4
1			5	6		7*	8	12	9					2	4	11	10		3								5
1	12	5	6			7	8		9					2	4	11*	10		3								6
1	12	5	6			7	8		9					2	4	11*	10		3								7
1	12	5	6			7	8		9					2	4	11*	10		3								8
1	2*	5				7	8	9					10		4	11			3	6	12						9
1			5†	6		7	8	9		11	10				4	12			3*	2		14					10
1	3		5†	6	14	7	8	9		11		10				12				2		4*					11
1	12	5	6			7	8			14	11	10				9			3*	2		4†					12
1	14			6		6	8			11	7		10*	3†	4	12	9			2							13
1	12			6		6	8			11	7		10	3*	4	9				2							14
1	3*	5	6			2	8			11			10		12		9			4			7				15
1			5			7	8	9†		11			10*	2	4	12			3	6			14				16
1			5	6			8		11				10	12	4		9		3	2*			7				17
1			5	6		7	8	12	11				10	2*	4		9		3								18
1			11	5		2	8		7		12		10*		4		9		3	6							19
1			5	6		2	8		7*		12		10	3	4		9			11							20
1			5	6		2	8		7		12		10	3	4		9			11							21
1			5	6		2	8*		7					3	4	12	10			11							22
1			5	6		2		7†	8					3	4*	10	9		12	11	14						23
1			5	6		7*		9	12					2	4	11†	10		3	8	14						24
1			5*	6		2	8†		7	12			10		4	14	9		3	11							25
1			5	6		2		14	8†	12			10		4	11*	9		3	7							26
1			5	6		2	8†	14	7*				10		4	12	9		3	11							27
1	4		5			2	8			11						7	9		3	6							28
1	3	5	6			2	8*			11						7	9		4			12					29
1	3	5*	6	12	2		9			11					4	8†	10		7		14						30
1	3	5	6		2*		8			11		14			4	10	9		12	7							31
1			5	6			8						10		4	11	9		3	7				2			32
1			5	6			8			11					4	10	9		3	7				2			33
1			5†	6			8*			11				12	4	10	9		3	7	14			2			34
1			5	6						11*			8	12	4	10	9		3	7				2			35
1			5	6			8			11			10		4	8	9	12	3*	7				2			36
1			5	6			8			11			10*		4	8	9	12	3	7				2			37
1			5	6			12			14	11*		10†		4	8	9		3	7				2			38
1	3		5	6			8			12			10		4*	11	9			7				2			39
1	3		5	6			8			14	11		10†	12		7*	9			4				2			40
1	3		5	6			8						10		4	11	9			7				2			41
1	3*		5	6						11	7		10		4	8	9		12					2			42
1	3		5	6				12		11			10		4	8†	9*	14		7				2			43
	3		5	6				12		11†	7		10*	14		8	9			4				2	1		44
	3*		5	6			8			11†	7			14		10	9		12	4				2	1		45
	3		5	6			8			11					4	10	9*			7			12	2	1		46
43	3	16	41	44	2	30	34	7	11	22	21	1	27	16	37	29	39		24	36	2	2	15	3	1		
	6				2		1	7		4	8	2	2	6	1	6	2	4	4		5	2	2				
		1		2		2	10	3	1	2						9	14	2								8	

1994-95

1	Aug	13	(a)	Bristol C	D	0-0		11,127
2		20	(h)	Millwall	D	1-1	Goodman	17,296
3		27	(a)	Stoke C	W	1-0	Gray P	15,159
4		30	(h)	Grimsby T	D	2-2	Goodman (pen), Gray P	15,788
5	Sep	3	(h)	Wolves	D	1-1	Gray P	15,111
6		11	(a)	Middlesbrough	D	2-2	Russell 2	19,587
7		13	(a)	Sheffield U	D	0-0		15,239
8		17	(h)	Barnsley	W	2-0	Gray P, Goodman	16,145
9		24	(a)	Tranmere R	L	0-1		7,500
10	Oct	1	(h)	Southend U	L	0-1		15,520
11		8	(a)	West Brom A	W	3-1	Smith M, Gray P 2	13,717
12		15	(h)	Burnley	D	0-0		17,700
13		22	(a)	Reading	W	2-0	Melville, Gray P	10,757
14		29	(h)	Oldham A	D	0-0		17,252
15	Nov	1	(h)	Charlton A	D	1-1	Smith M	14,085
16		5	(a)	Notts Co	L	2-3	Gray P, Owers	8,890
17		19	(h)	Watford	L	1-3	Smith M	15,063
18		26	(a)	Portsmouth	W	4-1	Russell, Melville, Gray P (pen), Smith M	7,527
19		29	(a)	Port Vale	D	0-0		8,121
20	Dec	3	(h)	Reading	L	0-1		14,021
21		10	(a)	Millwall	L	0-2		7,698
22		17	(h)	Bristol C	W	2-0	Howey 2	11,661
23		26	(h)	Bolton W	D	1-1	Smith M	19,758
24		27	(a)	Luton T	L	0-3		8,953
25		31	(h)	Derby Co	D	1-1	Gray P	139,799
26	Jan	14	(a)	Oldham A	D	0-0		9,742
27		21	(h)	Notts Co	L	1-2	Armstrong	14,334
28	Feb	4	(h)	Port Vale	D	1-1	Ball	13,377
29		11	(a)	Charlton A	L	0-1		12,380
30		18	(h)	Portsmouth	D	2-2	Smith M 2	12,372
31		21	(a)	Watford	W	1-0	Russell	8,189
32		25	(a)	Southend U	W	1-0	Agnew	4,686
33	Mar	5	(h)	Tranmere R	L	0-1		12,043
34		8	(a)	Wolves	L	0-1		25,926
35		11	(h)	Stoke C	W	1-0	Melville	12,282
36		15	(a)	Swindon T	L	0-1		8,233
37		19	(a)	Grimsby T	L	1-3	Agnew	5,697
38		21	(h)	Middlesbrough	L	0-1		16,501
39		25	(a)	Barnsley	L	0-2		7,803
40	Apr	1	(h)	Sheffield U	W	1-0	Russell	17,259
41		8	(a)	Derby Co	W	1-0	Ball	15,442
42		15	(h)	Luton T	D	1-1	Gray 2	17,292
43		17	(a)	Bolton W	L	0-1		15,030
44		22	(h)	Swindon T	W	1-0	Smith M	16,874
45		29	(a)	Burnley	D	1-1	Smith M	15,121
46	May	7	(h)	West Brom A	D	2-2	Smith M, Gray P	18,232

FINAL LEAGUE POSITION: 20th in Division One

Appearances

Sub. Appearances

Goals

Norman	Kubicki	Martin	Bennett	Ferguson	Melville	Owers	Goodman	Gray P	Gray Mi.	Ball	Atkinson	Cunnington	Ord	Russell	Smith M	Rodgerson	Chamberlain	Snodin	Howey	Armstrong	Scott	Agnew	Williams	Brodie	Matteo	Angell	Smith A	#
1	2	3*	4	5	6	7	8	9	10	11	12																	1
1	3		4	5*	6	2	8	9	10	11	7	12																2
1	3		4	5	6	2	8	9	10*	11	7	12																3
1	3		4*	5	6	2	8	9	10	11	7	12																4
1	3			5		2	8	9	10	6	7		4	11														5
1	2			5	6	7	8	9	12	4	11†	14	3	10*														6
1	2	12	5	6	7	8	9			4		11*	3	10														7
1	2	4*	5	6	7	8	9			11			3	10	12													8
1	2	5			6	7	8	9		4			3	10		11												9
1	2	5*			6	7	8	9		4			3	11	10	12	15											10
	2	5	4		6		8	9		7			3	11*	10	12	1											11
	2	5*			6		8	9		7			3	11	10		1	4		12								12
	2	5			6		8	9		7			3	11*	10	12	1	4										13
	2	5*			6	12	8	9		7			3	11	10		1	4†		14								14
	2	12			6	7	8	9		5			3	14	10	11*	1	4†										15
	2				6	7	8	9		5			3	12	10*	11	1	4										16
	2				6	7	8	9		5	11*		3†	12			1	4		14								17
	2	5			6	7		9		4	11		3	8	10		1											18
	2	5			6	7	12	9		4	11		3	8*	10		1											19
	2	5			6	7*		9		4	11†		3	8	10		1			14	12							20
	2	5	4			7		9*		6			3	8	10		1			12	11							21
	3		4	7	6	2		12		5				8	10		1		9	11*								22
	2	12	4	7*	6			9		5				8	10		1			11	3							23
	2	5			6			9		4	7	11*		8	10		1			12	3							24
	2	4			6			9	12	5	7*			8	10		1			11	3							25
	2		5		6			9	12	4				8	10		1			11*	3	7						26
	2	4	5		6			9							10		1		12	11	3	7*	8					27
1	2		5		6			9		4			12		10					11*	3	7	8					28
1	2	6	5*					9	12	11			4	8						14	3	7	10†					29
1	2		5					9*	8	4			6	12	10					11	3	7						30
1	2		5	6				9		4			7	8*	10†					12	3	11	14					31
1	2		4	5				9		11			6	8*	10†					12	3	7	14					32
1	2		4	5				9*		6			11	8	10					12	3	7						33
1	2		4	5						6			11	8	10*				9		3	7	12					34
1	2*		5	6						4				8	10				9	11	3	7	12					35
1	2	4*	5	6				9		11					10†				8		3	7	14					36
1	2		5	6				9		4		12	11†	8					10*		3	7	14					37
1	2			6				9		4		5†	11	8*					12	10	3	7	14					38
1	2	12†		6				9		4			4	14	10				11*		3	7		5	8			39
1	2	12	4	5*				9		11			6	14	10						3	7				8†		40
1	2	12	4					5		11			6	8	10						3	7*				9		41
1	2	7	4†					9	14	5	11		6	12	10						3					8*		42
1	2	10			6			9	5	7	11*		4	14	12						3					8†		43
1	2	7			6			9	5	11			4*		10						3					8	12	44
1	2	7			6			9*	5	11			4	12	10						3					8		45
1	2	5			6			12		4	7		11		10						3		9*			8		46
29	46	17	19	23	36	18	17	41	10	42	16	3	33	28	33	3	17	6	6	10	24	16	3	1	1	8		
5	1			1	1	1	6		1	5			10	2	3	1		9	5			7				8	1	
			3		1		3	12		2				5	10				2	1		2						

61

1995-96

1	Aug	12	(h)	Leicester C	L	1-2	Agnew	18,593
2		19	(a)	Norwich C	D	0-0		16,700
3		26	(h)	Wolves	W	2-0	Melville, Gray P	16,816
4		30	(a)	Port Vale	D	1-1	Gray P	7,693
5	Sep	2	(a)	Ipswich T	L	0-3		12,390
6		9	(h)	Southend U	W	1-0	Russell	13,805
7		12	(h)	Portsmouth	D	1-1	Melville	12,282
8		16	(a)	Luton T	W	2-0	Mullin, Gray P	6,955
9		23	(a)	Millwall	W	2-1	Scott (pen), Smith	8,691
10		30	(h)	Reading	D	2-2	Kelly, Melville	17,503
11	Oct	7	(a)	Crystal Palace	W	1-0	Kelly	13,754
12		14	(h)	Watford	D	1-1	Scott	17,970
13		21	(a)	Huddersfield T	D	1-1	Gray P	16,054
14		28	(h)	Barnsley	W	2-1	Russell, Howey	17,024
15	Nov	5	(a)	Charlton A	D	1-1	Gray Michael	11,626
16		18	(h)	Sheffield U	W	2-0	Gray P 2	16,640
17		22	(a)	Stoke C	L	0-1		11,754
18		25	(a)	West Brom A	W	1-0	Howey	15,931
19	Dec	3	(h)	Crystal Palace	W	1-0	Scott (pen)	12,777
20		9	(h)	Millwall	W	6-0	Scott (pen), Russell 4, Gray P	18,951
21		16	(a)	Reading	D	1-1	Smith	9,431
22		23	(a)	Derby Co	L	1-3	Gray Michael	16,882
23	Jan	14	(h)	Norwich C	L	0-1		14,983
24		21	(a)	Leicester C	D	0-0		16,130
25		24	(h)	Grimsby T	W	1-0	Ord	14,656
26		30	(h)	Tranmere R	D	0-0		17,616
27	Feb	3	(a)	Wolves	L	0-3		26,537
28		10	(h)	Port Vale	D	0-0		15,954
29		17	(a)	Portsmouth	D	2-2	Agnew, Howey	12,241
30		20	(h)	Ipswich T	W	1-0	Russell	14,052
31		24	(h)	Luton T	W	1-0	James (og)	16,693
32		27	(a)	Southend U	W	2-0	Scott (pen), Bridges	5,786
33	Mar	3	(a)	Grimsby T	W	4-0	Ball, Russell, Gray P, Bridges	5,318
34		9	(h)	Derby Co	W	3-0	Russell 2, Agnew	21,644
35		12	(a)	Oldham A	W	2-1	Gray Michael, Ball	7,149
36		17	(a)	Birmingham C	W	2-0	Agnew, Melville	23,250
37		23	(h)	Oldham A	W	1-0	Scott	20,631
38		30	(h)	Huddersfield T	W	3-2	Ball, Bridges 2	20,131
39	Apr	2	(a)	Watford	D	3-3	Agnew, Ball, Russell	11,195
40		6	(a)	Barnsley	W	1-0	Russell	13,189
41		8	(h)	Charlton A	D	0-0		20,914
42		13	(a)	Sheffield U	D	0-0		20,050
43		16	(h)	Birmingham C	W	3-0	Gray Michael, Stewart, Russell	19,831
44		21	(h)	Stoke C	D	0-0		21,276
45		27	(h)	West Brom A	D	0-0		22,027
46	May	5	(a)	Tranmere R	L	0-1		16,193

FINAL LEAGUE POSITION: 1st in Division One

Appearances

Sub. Appearances

Goals

Chamberlain	Kubicki	Scott	Bracewell	Ball	Ord	Gray Mi.	Agnew	Smith	Gray P	Angell	Russell	Armstrong	Gray Ma.	Atkinson	Howey	Melville	Mullin	Stewart	Aiston	Kelly	Hall	Given	Cooke	Bridges	
1	2	3	4	5	6	7	8†	9	10	11*	12	13													1
1	2		4	5	6	7		9*	10	11†	12		3	8	13										2
1	2	3	4	5		7		12	10†	11*				8	9	6	13								3
1	2	3	4	5		7*		12	10	11				8†	9	6		13							4
1	2	3	4	5	12	7°			10	11†					9	6	13		8*	14					5
1	2	3	4	5	8	7*		12†	10	11			14	9°		6		13							6
1	2	3	4	5	8	7			10	11*						6	9	12							7
1	2	3	4	5	8	7		12	10	11*					13	6	9†								8
1	2	3	4		8	7		12	10				11			6	9*		5						9
1	2	3	4	14	8°	7		13	10	12			11*			6	9†		5						10
1	2	3	4	8	9	11		7*	10	12						6			5						11
1	2	3	4	5	8	7		11†	10	12						6	9†	13							12
1	2	3	4	5*	9	7	12		10	13				14		6			11†	8°					13
1	2	3	4	5	8	7	12		10	9†					13	6			11*						14
1	2	3	4	5	8	7			10	11*						6		12	9						15
1	2	3	4	5	8	7		12	10	11*						6			9						16
1	2	3	4†	5	8	7		13	10	11*				12		6			14	9°					17
1	2	3		5	8	7	4	12	10						9	6			11*						18
1	2	3		5	8	7	4	11†	12					13	9*	6				10					19
1	2	3			8	7	4	11	10		9			5		6									20
1	2	3			8	7	4	11	10		9			5		6									21
1	2	3			8	7	4°	11†	10		9			5*		6			13	12	14				22
1	2*	3	4			8	7	5	13	10	9			12		6			11†						23
	2	3	4*			8	7*	5		10	9†		12		13	6					11	1			24
	2	3				8	7	5		10	9		12			6	13	11†		4		1			25
	2	3				8	7	5*		10	9		12			6				4		1	11		26
	2	3	4*			8	7	12		10	9					6	13			5		1	11		27
	2	3	4	5		7	10†			9				8		6						1	11	12	28
	2		4	5		7*	10	10*		9				8		6	13			3		1	11†	14	29
	2		4	5	8	7	12		9°						10	6				3		1	11		30
	2	3	4	5	8	7				9					10*	6						1	11	12	31
	2	3	4	5	8	7	11	10		9*						6						1	12		32
	2	3	4	5	8	7	11*	10		9†						6				12		1	13		33
	2	3	4	5	8	7†	11	12		9						6		10*		13		1			34
	2	3	4	5	8	7	11			9						6		10				1			35
	2	3	4	5	8	7	11	12†		9°						6		10*		13		1	14		36
	2	3	4	5	8	7	11			9*				12		6		10†				1	13		37
	2	3	4	5	8	7	11			9*						6		10				1	12		38
	2	3	4	5	8	7	11*			9†						6		10		12		1	13		39
	2	3	4	5	8	7	11			9*					13	6		10				1	12†		40
1	2	3	4	5	8	7	11†							12		6		10	13				9*		41
1	2	3	4	5	8	7	11			9*						6		10					12		42
1	2	3	4	5	8	7	11			9						6		10							43
1	2	3*	4	5	8	7	11†			9°					10	6			13	12			14		44
1	2	3	4		8	7	11			9					10*	6				5			12		45
1	2	3		5	8	7*	11	12		9						6			13	4				10†	46
29	46	43	38	35	41	46	26	9	28	2	35		4	5	17	40	5	11	4	9	8	17	6	2	
			1	1		3	11	4		6	1	3	2	10		5	1	10	1	3			13		
		6		4	1	4	5	2	8		13				3	4	1	1		2			4		

63

F.A. CUP

1971/72 SEASON
3rd Round
Jan 15 vs Sheffield Wednesday (h) 3-0
Att: 25,310 Porterfield, Watson, Chambers
4th Round
Feb 9 vs Cardiff City (a) 1-1
Att: 27,000 Chambers
Replay
Feb 14 vs Cardiff City (h) 1-1 (aet)
Att: 39,348 Kerr
2nd Replay (at Maine Road)
Feb 16 vs Cardiff City 1-3
Att: 8,868 McGiven

1972/73 SEASON
3rd Round
Jan 13 vs Notts County (a) 1-1
Att: 15,142 Watson
Replay
Jan 16 vs Notts County (h) 2-0
Att: 30,033 Watson, Tueart
4th Round
Feb 3 vs Reading (h) 1-1
Att: 33,913 Tueart
Replay
Feb 7 vs Reading (a) 3-1
Att: 19,793 Watson, Tueart, Kerr
5th Round
Feb 24 vs Manchester City (a) 2-2
Att: 54,478 Horswill, Hughes
Replay
Feb 27 vs Manchester City (h) 3-1
Att: 51,782 Halom, Hughes 2
6th Round
Mar 17 vs Luton Town (h) 2-0
Att: 53,151 Watson, Guthrie
Semi-Final (at Hillsborough)
Apr 7 vs Arsenal 2-1
Att: 55,000 Halom, Hughes
FINAL (at Wembley)
May 5 vs Leeds United 1-0
Att: 100,000 Porterfield

1973/74 SEASON
3rd Round
Jan 5 vs Carlisle United (a) 0-0
Att: 20,595
Replay
Jan 9 vs Carlisle United (h) 0-1
Att: 25,710

1974/75 SEASON
3rd Round
Jan 4 vs Chesterfield (h) 2-0
Att: 34,268 Bolton, Robson
4th Round
Jan 25 vs Middlesbrough (a) 1-3
Att: 39,400 Robson

1975/76 SEASON
3rd Round
Jan 3 vs Oldham Athletic (h) 2-0
Att: 29,226 Holden, Robson
4th Round
Feb 2 vs Hull City (h) 1-0
Att: 32,320 Finney
5th Round
Feb 14 vs Stoke City (a) 0-0
Att: 41,176
Replay
Feb 17 vs Stoke City (h) 2-1
Att: 47,583 Holden, Robson

6th Round
Mar 6 vs Crystal Palace (h) 0-1
Att: 50,850

1976/77 SEASON
3rd Round
Jan 8 vs Wrexham (h) 2-2
Att: 23,356 Holton, Holden
Replay
Jan 12 vs Wrexham (a) 0-1
Att: 16,023

1977/78 SEASON
3rd Round
Jan 7 vs Bristol Rovers (h) 0-1
Att: 26,574

1978/79 SEASON
3rd Round
Jan 10 vs Everton (h) 2-1
Att: 28,602 Rowell (pen), Lee
4th Round
Feb 21 vs Burnley (a) 1-1
Att: 20,000 Entwhistle
Replay
Feb 26 vs Burnley (h) 0-3
Att: 37,507

1979/80 SEASON
3rd Round
Jan 5 vs Bolton Wanderers (h) 0-1
Att: 24,464

1980/81 SEASON
3rd Round
Jan 3 vs Birmingham City (a) 1-1
Att: 23,098 Chisholm
Replay
Jan 7 vs Birmingham City (h) 1-2 (aet)
Att: 27,793 Rowell

1981/82 SEASON
3rd Round
Jan 2 vs Rotherham United (a) 1-1
Att: 11,649 Rowell
Replay
Jan 18 vs Rotherham United (h) 1-0
Att: 14,863 Buckley
4th Round
Jan 23 vs Liverpool (h) 0-3
Att: 28,582

1982/83 SEASON
3rd Round
Jan 8 vs Manchester City (h) 0-0
Att: 21,581
Replay
Jan 12 vs Manchester City (a) 1-2
Att: 22,356 Chisholm

1983/84 SEASON
3rd Round
Jan 7 vs Bolton Wanderers (a) 3-0
Att: 14,018
4th Round
Jan 28 vs Birmingham City (h) 1-2
Att: 21,226 West

1984/85 SEASON
3rd Round
Jan 5 vs Southampton (a) 0-4
Att: 15,516

1985/86 SEASON
3rd Round
Jan 4 vs Newport County (h) 2-0
Att: 12,352 Burley, Corner

4th Round
Jan 25 vs Manchester United (h) 0-0
Att: 35,484
Replay
Jan 29 vs Manchester United (a) 0-3
Att: 43,402

1986/87 SEASON
3rd Round
Jan 10 vs Wimbledon (a) 1-2
Att: 6,231 Gates

1987/88 SEASON
1st Round
Nov 14 vs Darlington (h) 2-0
Att: 16,892 Atkinson 2
2nd Round
Dec 5 vs Scunthorpe United (a) 1-2
Att: 7,178 Gates

1988/89 SEASON
3rd Round
Jan 7 vs Oxford United (h) 1-1
Att: 17,074 Ord
Replay
Jan 11 vs Oxford United (a) 0-2
Att: 7,236

1989/90 SEASON
3rd Round
Jan 6 vs Reading (a) 1-2
Att: 9,344 Armstrong

1990/91 SEASON
3rd Round
Jan 5 vs Arsenal (a) 1-2
Att: 35,128 O'Leary (og)

1991/92 SEASON
3rd Round
Jan 4 vs Port Vale (h) 3-0
Att: 15,564 Davenport, Byrne, Atkinson
4th Round
Jan 25 vs Oxford United (a) 3-2
Att: 9,968 Byrne, Hardyman, Atkinson
5th Round
Feb 15 vs West Ham United (h) 1-1
Att: 25,475 Byrne
Replay
Feb 26 vs West Ham United (a) 3-2
Att: 25,830 Byrne 2, Rush
6th Round
Mar 10 vs Chelsea (h) 1-1
Att: 33,948 Byrne
Replay
Mar 18 vs Chelsea (h) 2-1
Att: 26,089 Davenport, Armstrong
Semi-Final (at Hillsborough)
Apr 5 vs Norwich City 1-0
Att: 40,102 Byrne
FINAL (at Wembley)
May 9 vs Liverpool 0-2
Att: 79,544

1992/93 SEASON
3rd Round
Jan 12 vs Notts County (h) 2-0
Att: 8,522 Cunnington, Goodman
4th Round
Jan 24 vs Sheffield Wednesday (a) 0-1
Att: 33,422

1993/94 SEASON
3rd Round
Jan 8 vs Carlisle United (h) 1-1
Att: 23,587 Ferguson

Replay
Jan 18 vs Carlisle United (a) 1-0 (aet)
Att: 12,771 Howey

4th Round
Jan 29 vs Wimbledon (a) 1-2
Att: 10,477 Smith

1994/95 SEASON
3rd Round
Jan 7 vs Carlisle United (h) 1-1
Att: 15,523 Russell

Replay
Jan 17 vs Carlisle United (a) 3-1
Att: 12,201 Armstrong 2, Gray P

4th Round
Jan 29 vs Tottenham Hotspur (h) 1-4
Att: 21,135 Gray P

1995/96 SEASON
3rd Round
Jan 6 vs Manchester United (a) 2-2
Att: 41,563 Agnew, Russell

Replay
Jan 16 vs Manchester United (h) 1-2
Att: 21,378 Gray P

LEAGUE CUP
1971/72 SEASON
2nd Round
Sep 7 vs Bristol Rovers (a) 1-3
Att: 15,262 Hughes (pen)

1972/73 SEASON
2nd Round
Sep 6 vs Stoke City (a) 0-3
Att: 17,600

1973/74 SEASON
2nd Round
Oct 8 vs Derby County (a) 2-2
Att: 29,172 Lathan 2

Replay
Oct 29 vs Derby County (h) 1-1 (aet)
Att: 38,975 Tueart

2nd Replay
Oct 31 vs Derby County (h) 3-0
Att: 38,460 Halom 3

3rd Round
Nov 21 vs Liverpool (h) 0-2
Att: 36,208

1974/75 SEASON
2nd Round
Sep 10 vs Preston North End (a) 0-2
Att: 13,279

1975/76 SEASON
2nd Round
Sep 9 vs Notts County (a) 1-2
Att: 12,500 Holden

1976/77 SEASON
2nd Round
Aug 31 vs Luton Town (h) 3-1
Att: 22,390 Hughes 2, Robson

3rd Round
Sep 21 vs Manchester United (a) 2-2
Att: 46,170 Train, Towers

Replay
Oct 4 vs Manchester United (h) 2-2
Att: 30,831 Towers (pen), Train

2nd Replay
Oct 6 vs Manchester United (a) 0-1
Att: 47,689

1977/78 SEASON
2nd Round
Aug 30 vs Middlesbrough (h) 2-2
Att: 26,597 Holden, Rowell

Replay
Sep 13 vs Middlesbrough (a) 0-1
Att: 29,572

1978/79 SEASON
2nd Round
Aug 30 vs Stoke City (h) 0-2
Att: 12,368

1979/80 SEASON
2nd Round (1st leg)
Aug 29 vs Newcastle United (h) 2-2
Att: 27,658 Robson (pen), Rostron

2nd Round (2nd leg)
Sep 15 vs Newcastle U (a) 2-2 (aet)(agg 4-4)
Att: 30,553 Brown 2
Sunderland won 7-6 on penalties

3rd Round
Sep 26 vs Manchester City (a) 1-1
Att: 26,181 Chisholm

Replay
Oct 3 vs Manchester City (h) 1-0
Att: 33,559 Robson

4th Round
Oct 31 vs West Ham United (h) 1-1
Att: 30,302 Brown

Replay
Nov 5 vs West Ham United (a) 1-2
Att: 30,302 Brown

1980/81 SEASON
2nd Round (1st leg)
Aug 27 vs Stockport County (a) 1-1
Att: 6,108 Arnott

2nd Round (2nd leg)
Sep 3 vs Stockport County (h) 1-2 (agg. 2-3)
Att: 17,346 Cummins

1981/82 SEASON
2nd Round (1st leg)
Oct 7 vs Rotherham United (h) 2-0
Att: 10,450 Rowell (pen), Ritchie

2nd Round (2nd leg)
Oct 27 vs Rotherham Utd. (a) 3-3 (agg. 5-3)
Att: 8,179 Ritchie 2, Cummins

3rd Round
Nov 11 vs Crystal Palace (h) 0-1
At: 11,139

1982/83 SEASON
2nd Round (1st leg)
Oct 4 vs Wolverhampton Wanderers (a) 1-1
Att: 13,662 Rowell (pen)

2nd Round (2nd leg)
Oct 27 vs Wolverhampton (h) 5-0 (agg 6-1)
Att: 11,901 Chisholm 2, Hindmarch, Rowell, McCoist

3rd Round
Nov 10 vs Norwich City (h) 0-0
Att: 10,934

Replay
Nov 24 vs Norwich City (a) 1-3
Att: 19,776

1983/84 SEASON
2nd Round (1st leg)
Oct 4 vs Cambridge United (a) 3-2
Att: 4,835 Rowell 2, West

2nd Round (2nd leg)
Oct 26 vs Cambridge Utd. (h) 4-3 (agg. 7-5)
Att: 9,059 Rowell 2 (1 pen), Proctor, Cooke

3rd Round
Nov 9 vs Norwich City (a) 0-0
Att: 12,406

Replay
Nov 22 vs Norwich City (h) 1-2
Att: 14,149 West

1984/85 SEASON
2nd Round (1st leg)
Sep 25 vs Crystal Palace (h) 2-1
Att: 11,696 Wylde 2

2nd Round (2nd leg)
Oct 10 vs Crystal Palace (a) 0-0 (agg. 2-1)
Att: 6,871

3rd Round
Oct 31 vs Nottingham Forest (a) 1-1
Att: 14,291 Hodgson

Replay
Nov 6 vs Nottingham Forest (h) 1-0 (aet)
Att: 23,184 Gayle

4th Round
Nov 21 vs Tottenham Hotspur (h) 0-0
Att: 27,421

Replay
Dec 5 vs Tottenham Hotspur (a) 2-1
Att: 25,835 Walker, Chisholm

Quarter-Final
Jan 16 vs Watford (a) 1-0
Att: 22,591 Walker

Semi-Final (1st leg)
Feb 13 vs Chelsea (h) 2-0
Att: 32,440 West 2 (1 pen)

Semi-Final (2nd leg)
Mar 4 vs Chelsea (a) 3-2 (aggregate 5-2)
Att: 38,440 Walker 2, West

FINAL (at Wembley)
Mar 24 vs Norwich City 0-1
Att: 100,000

1985/86 SEASON
2nd Round (1st leg)
Sep 23 vs Swindon Town (h) 3-2
Att: 14,207 Walker, Gates (pen), Bennett

2nd Round (2nd leg)
Oct 7 vs Swindon Town (a) 1-3 (agg. 4-5)
Att: 9,111 Walker

1986/87 SEASON
1st Round (1st leg)
Aug 26 vs York City (h) 2-4
Att: 9,162 Buchanan, Gates

1st Round (2nd leg)
Sep 2 vs York City (a) 3-1 (aggregate 5-5)
Att: 6,480 Buchanan 2, Proctor
York City won on the Away Goals rule

1987/88 SEASON
1st Round (1st leg)
Aug 18 vs Middlesbrough (h) 1-0
Att: 15,770 Gates

1st Round (2nd leg)
Aug 25 vs Middlesbrough (a) 0-2 (agg. 1-2)
Att: 15,571

1988/89 SEASON
1st Round (1st leg)
Aug 30 vs York City (a) 0-0
Att: 4,204

1st Round (2nd leg)
Sep 6 vs York City (h) 4-0 (aggregate 4-0)
Att: 9,388 Gabbiadini 2, Pascoe 2

2nd Round (1st leg)
Sep 27 vs West Ham United (h) 0-3
Att: 13,691

2nd Round (2nd leg)
Oct 12 vs West Ham United (a) 1-2 (agg 1-5)
Att: 10,558 Gabbiadini

1989/90 SEASON
2nd Round (1st leg)
Sep 19 vs Fulham (h) 1-1
Att: 11,416 Hardyman (pen)

2nd Round (2nd leg)
Oct 3 vs Fulham (a) 3-0 (aggregate 4-1)
Att: 6,314 Gabbiadini 2, Armstrong

3rd Round
Oct 24 vs Bournemouth (h) 1-1
Att: 12,595 Gabbiadini

Replay
Nov 7 vs Bournemouth (a) 1-0
Att: 7,349 Gabbiadini

4th Round
Nov 29 vs Exeter City (a) 2-2
Att: 8,643 Armstrong, Gates

Replay
Dec 5 vs Exeter City (h) 5-2
Att: 18,130 Pascoe, Armstrong, Gates 2, Hardyman (pen)

5th Round
Jan 17 vs Coventry City (h) 0-0
Att: 27,218

Replay
Jan 24 vs Coventry City (a) 0-5
Att: 21,219

1990/91 SEASON
2nd Round (1st leg)
Sep 25 vs Bristol City (h) 0-1
Att: 10,358

2nd Round (2nd leg)
Oct 9 vs Bristol City (a) 6-1 (aggregate 6-2)
Att: 11,776 Hauser, Ball, Owers, Gabbiadini 2, Cullen

3rd Round
Oct 31 vs Derby County (a) 0-6
Att: 16,422

1991/92 SEASON
2nd Round (1st leg)
Sep 24 vs Huddersfield Town (h) 1-2
Att: 8,161 Hauser

2nd Round (2nd leg)
Oct 9 vs Huddersfield Tn. (a) 0-4 (agg 1-6)
Att: 11,177

1992/93 SEASON
1st Round (1st leg)
Aug 18 vs Huddersfield Town (h) 2-3
Att: 10,726 Butcher, Ball

1st Round (2nd leg)
Aug 26 vs Huddersfield Town (a) 1-0 (aet)
(aggregate 3-3)
Att: 6,737 Davenport
Huddersfield won on the Away Goals rule

1993/94 SEASON
1st Round (1st leg)
Aug 17 vs Chester City (h) 3-1
Att: 9,484 Goodman 2, Power

1st Round (2nd leg)
Aug 24 vs Chester City (a) 0-0 (aggreg. 3-1)
Att: 2,903

2nd Round (1st leg)
Sep 21 vs Leeds United (h) 2-1
Att: 17,101 Goodman, Gray P

2nd Round (2nd leg)
Oct 6 vs Leeds United (a) 2-1 (aggreg. 4-2)
Att: 22,265 Goodman, Gray P

3rd Round
Oct 26 vs Aston Villa (h) 1-4
Att: 23,692 Gray P

1994/95 SEASON
2nd Round (1st leg)
Sep 20 vs Millwall (a) 1-2
Att: 5,095 Russell

2nd Round (2nd leg)
Oct 4 vs Millwall (h) 1-1 (aggregate 2-3)
Att: 9,698 Gray P

1995/96 SEASON
1st Round (1st leg)
Aug 14 vs Preston North End (a) 1-1
Att: 6,323 Angell

1st Round (2nd leg)
Aug 23 vs Preston N.E. (h) 3-2 (aggreg. 4-3)
Att: 7,407 Howey 2, Kidd (og)

2nd Round (1st leg)
Sep 19 vs Liverpool (a) 0-2
Att: 25,579

2nd Round (2nd leg)
Oct 4 vs Liverpool (h) 0-1 (aggregate 0-3)
Att: 20,560

EUROPEAN CUP-WINNERS-CUP
1973/74 SEASON
1st Round (1st leg)
Sep 19 vs Vasas Budapest (a) 2-0
Att: 35,000 Hughes, Tueart

1st Round (2nd leg)
Oct 3 vs Vasas Budapest (h) 1-0 (agg. 3-0)
Att: 22,762 Tueart (pen)

2nd Round (1st leg)
Oct 24 vs Sporting Lisbon (h) 2-1
Att: 31,568 Kerr, Horswill

2nd Round (2nd leg)
Nov 7 vs Sporting Lisbon (a) 0-2 (agg. 2-3)
Att: 50,000

1971-72 SEASON

SECOND DIVISION

Norwich City	42	21	15	6	60	36	57
Birmingham City	42	19	18	5	60	31	56
Millwall	42	19	17	6	64	46	55
Q.P.R.	42	20	14	8	57	28	54
Sunderland	**42**	**17**	**16**	**9**	**67**	**57**	**50**
Blackpool	42	20	7	15	70	50	47
Burnley	42	20	6	16	70	55	46
Bristol City	42	18	10	14	61	49	46
Middlesbrough	42	19	8	15	50	48	46
Carlisle United	42	17	9	16	61	57	43
Swindon Town	42	15	12	15	47	47	42
Hull City	42	14	10	18	49	53	38
Luton Town	42	10	18	14	43	48	38
Sheffield Wednesday	42	13	12	17	51	58	38
Oxford United	42	12	14	16	43	55	38
Portsmouth	42	12	13	17	59	68	37
Orient	42	14	9	19	50	61	37
Preston North End	42	12	12	18	52	58	36
Cardiff City	42	10	14	18	56	69	34
Fulham	42	12	10	20	45	68	34
Charlton Athletic	42	12	9	21	55	77	33
Watford	42	5	9	28	24	75	19

1972-73 SEASON

SECOND DIVISION

Burnley	42	24	14	4	72	35	62
Q.P.R.	42	24	13	5	81	37	61
Aston Villa	42	18	14	10	51	47	50
Middlesbrough	42	17	13	12	46	43	47
Bristol City	42	17	12	13	63	51	46
Sunderland	**42**	**17**	**12**	**13**	**59**	**49**	**46**
Blackpool	42	18	10	14	56	51	46
Oxford United	42	19	7	16	52	43	45
Fulham	42	16	12	14	58	49	44
Sheffield Wednesday	42	17	10	15	59	55	44
Millwall	42	16	10	16	55	47	42
Luton Town	42	15	11	16	44	43	41
Hull City	42	14	12	16	64	49	40
Nottingham Forest	42	14	12	16	47	52	40
Orient	42	12	12	18	49	53	36
Swindon Town	42	10	16	16	46	60	36
Portsmouth	42	12	11	19	42	59	35
Carlisle United	42	11	12	19	50	52	34
Preston North End	42	11	12	19	37	64	34
Cardiff City	42	11	11	20	43	58	33
Huddersfield Town	42	8	17	17	36	56	33
Brighton & Hove Alb.	42	8	13	21	46	83	29

1973-74 SEASON

SECOND DIVISION

Middlesbrough	42	27	11	4	77	30	65
Luton Town	42	19	12	11	64	51	50
Carlisle United	42	20	9	13	61	48	49
Orient	42	15	18	9	55	42	48
Blackpool	42	17	13	12	57	40	47
Sunderland	**42**	**19**	**9**	**14**	**58**	**44**	**47**
Nottingham Forest	42	15	15	12	57	43	45
West Brom. Albion	42	14	16	12	48	45	44
Hull City	42	13	17	12	46	47	43
Notts County	42	15	13	14	55	60	43
Bolton Wanderers	42	15	12	15	44	40	42
Millwall	42	14	14	14	51	51	42
Fulham	42	16	10	16	39	43	42
Aston Villa	42	13	15	14	48	45	41
Portsmouth	42	14	12	16	45	62	40
Bristol City	42	14	10	18	47	54	38
Cardiff City	42	10	16	16	49	62	36
Oxford United	42	10	16	16	35	46	36
Sheffield Wednesday	42	12	11	19	51	63	35
Crystal Palace	42	11	12	19	43	56	34
Preston North End *	42	9	14	19	40	62	31
Swindon Town	42	7	11	24	36	72	25

* Preston - one point deducted for fielding ineligible player

1974-75 SEASON

SECOND DIVISION

Manchester United	42	26	9	7	66	30	61
Aston Villa	42	25	8	9	69	32	58
Norwich City	42	20	13	9	58	37	53
Sunderland	**42**	**19**	**13**	**10**	**65**	**35**	**51**
Bristol City	42	21	8	13	47	33	50
West Brom. Albion	42	18	9	15	54	42	45
Blackpool	42	14	17	11	38	33	45
Hull City	42	15	14	13	40	53	44
Fulham	42	13	16	13	44	39	42
Bolton	42	15	12	15	45	41	42
Oxford United	42	15	12	15	41	51	42
Orient	42	11	20	11	28	39	42
Southampton	42	15	11	16	53	54	41
Notts County	42	12	16	14	49	59	40
York City	42	14	10	18	51	55	38
Nottingham Forest	42	12	14	16	43	55	38
Portsmouth	42	12	13	17	44	54	37
Oldham Athletic	42	10	15	17	40	48	35
Bristol Rovers	42	12	11	19	42	64	35
Millwall	42	10	12	20	44	56	32
Cardiff City	42	9	14	19	36	62	32
Sheffield Wednesday	42	5	11	26	29	64	21

1975-76 SEASON

SECOND DIVISION

Sunderland	**42**	**24**	**8**	**10**	**67**	**36**	**56**
Bristol City	42	19	15	8	59	35	53
West Brom. Albion	42	20	13	9	50	33	53
Bolton Wanderers	42	20	12	10	64	38	52
Notts County	42	19	11	12	60	41	49
Southampton	42	21	7	14	66	50	49
Luton Town	42	19	10	13	61	51	48
Nottingham Forest	42	17	12	13	55	40	46
Charlton Athletic	42	15	12	15	61	72	42
Blackpool	42	14	14	14	40	49	42
Chelsea	42	12	16	14	53	54	40
Fulham	42	13	14	15	45	47	40
Orient	42	13	14	15	37	39	40
Hull City	42	14	11	17	45	49	39
Blackburn Rovers	42	12	14	16	45	50	38
Plymouth Argyle	42	13	12	17	48	54	38
Oldham Athletic	42	13	12	17	57	68	38
Bristol Rovers	42	11	16	15	38	50	38
Carlisle United	42	12	13	17	45	59	37
Oxford United	42	11	11	20	39	59	33
York City	42	10	8	24	39	71	28
Portsmouth	42	9	7	26	32	61	25

1976-77 SEASON

FIRST DIVISION

Liverpool	42	23	11	8	62	33	57
Manchester City	42	21	14	7	60	34	56
Ipswich Town	42	22	8	12	66	39	52
Aston Villa	42	22	7	13	76	50	51
Newcastle United	42	18	13	11	64	49	49
Manchester United	42	18	11	13	71	62	47
West Brom. Albion	42	16	13	13	62	56	45
Arsenal	42	16	11	15	64	59	43
Everton	42	14	14	14	62	64	42
Leeds United	42	15	12	15	48	51	42
Leicester City	42	12	18	12	47	60	42
Middlesbrough	42	14	13	15	40	45	41
Birmingham City	42	13	12	17	63	61	38
Q.P.R.	42	13	12	17	47	52	38
Derby County	42	9	19	14	50	55	37
Norwich City	42	14	9	19	47	64	37
West Ham United	42	11	14	17	46	65	36
Bristol City	42	11	13	18	38	48	35
Coventry City	42	10	15	17	48	59	35
Sunderland	**42**	**11**	**12**	**19**	**46**	**54**	**34**
Stoke City	42	10	14	18	28	51	34
Tottenham Hotspur	42	12	9	21	48	72	33

1977-78 SEASON

SECOND DIVISION

Bolton Wanderers	42	24	10	8	63	33	58
Southampton	42	22	13	7	70	39	57
Tottenham Hotspur	42	20	16	6	83	49	56
Brighton & Hove Alb.	42	22	12	8	63	38	56
Blackburn Rovers	42	16	13	13	56	60	45
Sunderland	**42**	**14**	**16**	**12**	**67**	**59**	**44**
Stoke City	42	16	10	16	53	49	42
Oldham Athletic	42	13	16	13	54	58	42
Crystal Palace	42	13	15	14	50	47	41
Fulham	42	14	13	15	49	49	41
Burnley	42	15	10	17	56	64	40
Sheffield United	42	16	8	18	62	73	40
Luton Town	42	14	10	18	54	52	38
Orient	42	10	18	14	43	49	38
Notts County	42	11	16	15	54	62	38
Millwall	42	12	14	16	49	57	38
Charlton Athletic	42	13	12	17	55	68	38
Bristol Rovers	42	13	12	17	61	77	38
Cardiff City	42	13	12	17	51	71	38
Blackpool	42	12	13	17	59	60	37
Mansfield Town	42	10	11	21	49	69	31
Hull City	42	8	12	22	34	52	28

1978-79 SEASON

SECOND DIVISION

Crystal Palace	42	19	19	4	51	24	57
Brighton & Hove Alb.	42	23	10	9	72	39	56
Stoke City	42	20	16	6	58	31	56
Sunderland	**42**	**22**	**11**	**9**	**70**	**44**	**55**
West Ham United	42	18	14	10	70	39	50
Notts County	42	14	16	12	48	60	44
Preston North End	42	12	18	12	59	57	42
Newcastle United	42	17	8	17	51	55	42
Cardiff City	42	16	10	16	56	70	42
Fulham	42	13	15	14	50	47	41
Orient	42	15	10	17	51	51	40
Cambridge United	42	12	16	14	44	52	40
Burnley	42	14	12	16	51	62	40
Oldham Athletic	42	13	13	16	52	61	39
Wrexham	42	12	14	16	45	42	38
Bristol Rovers	42	14	10	18	48	60	38
Leicester City	42	10	17	15	43	52	37
Luton Town	42	13	10	19	60	57	36
Charlton Athletic	42	11	13	18	60	69	35
Sheffield United	42	11	12	19	52	69	34
Millwall	42	11	10	21	42	61	32
Blackburn Rovers	42	10	10	22	41	72	30

1979-80 SEASON

SECOND DIVISION

Leicester City	42	21	13	8	58	38	55
Sunderland	**42**	**21**	**12**	**9**	**69**	**42**	**54**
Birmingham City	42	21	11	10	58	38	53
Chelsea	42	23	7	12	66	52	53
Q.P.R.	42	18	13	11	75	53	49
Luton Town	42	16	17	9	66	45	49
West Ham United	42	20	7	15	54	43	47
Cambridge United	42	14	16	12	61	53	44
Newcastle United	42	15	14	13	53	49	44
Preston North End	42	12	19	11	56	52	43
Oldham Athletic	42	16	11	15	49	53	43
Swansea City	42	17	9	16	48	53	43
Shrewsbury Town	42	18	5	19	60	53	41
Orient	42	12	17	13	48	54	41
Cardiff City	42	16	8	18	41	48	40
Wrexham	42	16	6	20	40	49	38
Notts County	42	11	15	16	51	52	37
Watford	42	12	13	17	39	46	37
Bristol Rovers	42	11	13	18	50	64	35
Fulham	42	11	7	24	42	74	29
Burnley	42	6	15	21	39	73	27
Charlton Athletic	42	6	10	26	39	78	22

1980-81 SEASON

FIRST DIVISION

Aston Villa	42	26	8	8	72	40	60
Ipswich Town	42	23	10	9	77	43	56
Arsenal	42	19	15	8	61	45	53
West Brom. Albion	42	20	12	10	60	42	52
Liverpool	42	17	17	8	62	46	51
Southampton	42	20	10	12	76	56	50
Nottingham Forest	42	19	12	11	62	45	50
Manchester United	42	15	18	9	51	36	48
Leeds United	42	17	10	15	39	47	44
Tottenham Hotspur	42	14	15	13	70	68	43
Stoke City	42	12	18	12	51	60	42
Manchester City	42	14	11	17	56	59	39
Birmingham City	42	13	12	17	50	61	38
Middlesbrough	42	16	5	21	53	51	37
Everton	42	13	10	19	55	58	36
Coventry City	42	13	10	19	48	68	36
Sunderland	**42**	**14**	**7**	**21**	**58**	**53**	**35**
Wolves	42	13	9	20	47	55	35
Brighton & Hove Alb.	42	14	7	21	54	67	35
Norwich City	42	13	7	22	49	73	33
Leicester City	42	13	6	23	40	67	32
Crystal Palace	42	6	7	29	47	83	19

1981-82 SEASON

FIRST DIVISION

Liverpool	42	26	9	7	80	32	87
Ipswich Town	42	26	5	11	75	53	83
Manchester United	42	22	12	8	59	29	78
Tottenham Hotspur	42	20	11	11	67	48	71
Arsenal	42	20	11	11	48	37	71
Swansea City	42	21	6	15	58	51	69
Southampton	42	19	9	14	72	67	66
Everton	42	17	13	12	56	50	64
West Ham United	42	14	16	12	66	57	58
Manchester City	42	15	13	14	49	50	58
Aston Villa	42	15	12	15	55	53	57
Nottingham Forest	42	15	12	15	42	48	57
Brighton & Hove Alb.	42	13	13	16	43	52	52
Coventry City	42	13	11	18	56	62	50
Notts County	42	13	8	21	45	69	47
Birmingham City	42	10	14	18	53	61	44
West Brom. Albion	42	11	11	20	46	57	44
Stoke City	42	12	8	22	44	63	44
Sunderland	**42**	**11**	**11**	**20**	**38**	**58**	**44**
Leeds United	42	10	12	20	39	61	42
Wolves	42	10	10	22	32	63	40
Middlesbrough	42	8	15	19	34	52	39

1982-83 SEASON

FIRST DIVISION

Liverpool	42	24	10	8	87	37	82
Watford	42	22	5	15	74	57	71
Manchester United	42	19	13	8	56	38	70
Tottenham Hotspur	42	20	9	13	65	50	69
Nottingham Forest	42	20	9	13	62	50	69
Aston Villa	42	21	5	16	62	50	68
Everton	42	18	10	14	66	48	64
West Ham United	42	20	4	18	68	62	64
Ipswich Town	42	15	13	14	64	50	58
Arsenal	42	16	10	16	58	56	58
West Brom. Albion	42	15	12	15	51	49	57
Southampton	42	15	12	15	54	58	57
Stoke City	42	16	9	17	53	64	57
Norwich City	42	14	12	16	52	58	54
Notts County	42	15	7	21	55	71	52
Sunderland	**42**	**12**	**14**	**16**	**48**	**61**	**50**
Birmingham City	42	12	15	16	40	55	50
Luton Town	42	12	13	17	65	84	49
Coventry City	42	13	9	20	48	59	48
Manchester City	42	13	8	21	47	70	47
Swansea City	42	10	11	21	51	69	41
Brighton & Hove Alb.	42	9	13	20	38	67	40

1983-84 SEASON

FIRST DIVISION

Liverpool	42	22	14	6	73	32	80
Southampton	42	22	11	9	66	38	77
Nottingham Forest	42	22	8	12	76	45	74
Manchester United	42	20	14	8	71	41	74
Q.P.R.	42	22	7	13	67	37	73
Arsenal	42	19	9	15	74	60	63
Everton	42	16	14	12	44	42	62
Tottenham Hotspur	42	17	10	15	64	65	61
West Ham United	42	17	9	16	60	55	60
Aston Villa	42	17	9	16	59	61	60
Watford	42	16	9	17	68	77	57
Ipswich Town	42	15	8	19	55	57	53
Sunderland	**42**	**13**	**13**	**16**	**42**	**53**	**52**
Norwich City	42	12	15	15	48	49	51
Leicester City	42	13	12	17	65	68	51
Luton Town	42	14	9	19	53	66	51
West Brom. Albion	42	14	9	19	48	62	51
Stoke City	42	13	11	18	44	63	50
Coventry City	42	13	11	18	57	77	50
Birmingham City	42	12	12	18	39	50	48
Notts County	42	10	11	21	50	72	41
Wolves	42	6	11	25	27	80	29

1984-85 SEASON

FIRST DIVISION

Everton	42	28	6	8	88	43	90
Liverpool	42	22	11	9	78	35	77
Tottenham Hotspur	42	23	8	11	78	51	77
Manchester United	42	22	10	10	77	47	76
Southampton	42	19	11	12	56	47	68
Chelsea	42	18	12	12	63	48	66
Arsenal	42	19	9	14	61	49	66
Sheffield Wednesday	42	17	14	11	58	45	65
Nottingham Forest	42	19	7	16	56	48	64
Aston Villa	42	15	11	16	60	60	56
Watford	42	14	13	15	81	71	55
West Brom	42	16	7	19	58	62	55
Luton Town	42	15	9	18	57	61	54
Newcastle United	42	13	13	16	55	70	52
Leicester City	42	15	6	21	65	73	51
West Ham United	42	13	12	17	51	68	51
Ipswich Town	42	13	11	18	46	57	50
Coventry City	42	15	5	22	47	64	50
QPR	42	13	11	18	53	72	50
Norwich City	42	13	10	19	46	64	49
Sunderland	**42**	**10**	**10**	**22**	**40**	**62**	**40**
Stoke City	42	3	8	31	24	91	17

1985-86 SEASON

SECOND DIVISION

Norwich City	42	25	9	8	84	39	84
Charlton Athletic	42	22	11	9	78	45	77
Wimbledon	42	21	13	8	58	37	76
Portsmouth	42	22	7	13	69	41	73
Crystal Palace	42	19	9	14	57	52	66
Hull City	42	17	13	12	65	55	64
Sheffield United	42	17	11	14	64	63	62
Oldham Athletic	42	17	9	16	62	61	60
Millwall	42	17	8	17	64	65	59
Stoke City	42	14	15	13	48	50	57
Brighton & Hove Alb.	42	16	8	18	64	64	56
Barnsley	42	14	14	14	47	50	56
Bradford City	42	16	6	20	51	63	54
Leeds United	42	15	8	19	56	72	53
Grimsby Town	42	14	10	18	58	62	52
Huddersfield Town	42	14	10	18	51	67	52
Shrewsbury Town	42	14	9	19	52	64	51
Sunderland	**42**	**13**	**11**	**18**	**47**	**61**	**50**
Blackburn Rovers	42	12	13	17	53	62	49
Carlisle United	42	13	7	22	47	71	46
Middlesbrough	42	12	9	21	44	53	45
Fulham	42	10	6	26	45	69	36

1986-87 SEASON

SECOND DIVISION

Derby County	42	25	9	8	64	38	84
Portsmouth	42	23	9	10	53	28	78
Oldham Athletic	42	22	9	11	65	44	75
Leeds United	42	19	11	12	58	44	68
Ipswich Town	42	17	13	12	59	43	64
Crystal Palace	42	19	5	18	51	53	62
Plymouth Argyle	42	16	13	13	62	57	61
Stoke City	42	16	10	16	63	53	58
Sheffield United	42	15	13	14	50	49	58
Bradford City	42	15	10	17	62	62	55
Barnsley	42	14	13	15	49	52	55
Blackburn Rovers	42	15	10	17	45	55	55
Reading	42	14	11	17	52	59	53
Hull City	42	13	14	15	41	55	53
West Brom	42	13	12	17	51	49	51
Millwall	42	14	9	19	39	45	51
Huddersfield Town	42	13	12	17	54	61	51
Shrewsbury Town	42	15	6	21	41	53	51
Birmingham City	42	11	17	14	47	59	50
Sunderland	**42**	**12**	**12**	**18**	**49**	**59**	**48**
Grimsby Town	42	10	14	18	39	59	44
Brighton & Hove Alb.	42	9	12	21	37	54	39

1987-88 SEASON

THIRD DIVISION

Sunderland	**46**	**27**	**12**	**7**	**92**	**48**	**93**
Brighton & Hove Alb.	46	23	15	8	69	47	84
Walsall	46	23	13	10	68	50	82
Notts County	46	23	12	11	82	49	81
Bristol City	46	21	12	13	77	62	75
Northampton Town	46	18	19	9	70	51	73
Wigan Athletic	46	20	12	14	70	61	72
Bristol Rovers	46	18	12	16	68	56	66
Fulham	46	19	9	18	69	60	66
Blackpool	46	17	14	15	71	62	65
Port Vale	46	18	11	17	58	56	65
Brentford	46	16	14	16	53	59	62
Gillingham	46	14	17	15	77	61	59
Bury	46	15	14	17	58	57	59
Chester City	46	14	16	16	51	62	58
Preston North End	46	15	13	18	48	59	58
Southend United	46	14	13	19	65	83	55
Chesterfield	46	15	10	21	41	70	55
Mansfield Town	46	14	12	20	48	59	54
Aldershot	46	15	8	23	64	74	53
Rotherham United	46	12	16	18	50	66	52
Grimsby Town	46	12	14	20	48	58	50
York City	46	8	9	29	48	91	33
Doncaster Rovers	46	8	9	29	40	84	3

1988-89 SEASON

SECOND DIVISION

Chelsea	46	29	12	5	96	50	99
Manchester City	46	23	13	10	77	53	82
Crystal Palace	46	23	12	11	71	49	81
Watford	46	22	12	12	74	48	78
Blackburn Rovers	46	22	11	13	74	59	77
Swindon Town	46	20	16	10	68	53	76
Barnsley	46	20	14	12	66	58	74
Ipswich Town	46	22	7	17	71	61	73
West Brom	46	18	18	10	65	41	72
Leeds United	46	17	16	13	59	50	67
Sunderland	**46**	**16**	**15**	**15**	**60**	**60**	**63**
Bournemouth	46	18	8	20	53	62	62
Stoke City	46	15	14	17	57	72	59
Bradford City	46	13	17	16	52	59	56
Leicester City	46	13	16	17	56	63	55
Oldham Athletic	46	11	21	14	75	72	54
Oxford United	46	14	12	20	62	70	54
Plymouth Argyle	46	14	12	20	55	66	54
Brighton & Hove Alb.	46	14	9	23	57	66	51
Portsmouth	46	13	12	21	53	62	51
Hull City	46	11	14	21	52	68	47
Shrewsbury Town	46	8	18	20	40	67	42
Birmingham City	46	8	11	27	31	76	35
Walsall	46	5	16	25	41	80	31

1989-90 SEASON

SECOND DIVISION

Leeds United	46	24	13	9	79	52	85
Sheffield United	46	24	13	9	78	58	85
Newcastle United	46	22	14	10	80	55	80
Swindon Town	46	20	14	12	79	59	74
Blackburn Rovers	46	19	17	10	74	59	74
Sunderland	**46**	**20**	**14**	**12**	**70**	**64**	**74**
West Ham United	46	20	12	14	80	57	72
Oldham Athletic	46	19	14	13	70	57	71
Ipswich Town	46	19	12	15	67	66	69
Wolves	46	18	13	15	67	60	67
Port Vale	46	15	16	15	62	57	61
Portsmouth	46	15	16	15	62	65	61
Leicester City	46	15	14	17	67	79	59
Hull City	46	14	16	16	58	65	58
Watford	46	14	15	17	58	60	57
Plymouth Argyle	46	14	13	19	58	63	55
Oxford United	46	15	9	22	57	66	54
Brighton & Hove Alb.	46	15	9	22	56	72	54
Barnsley	46	13	15	18	49	71	54
West Brom	46	12	15	19	67	71	51
Middlesbrough	46	13	11	22	52	63	50
Bournemouth	46	12	12	22	57	76	48
Bradford City	46	9	14	23	44	68	41
Stoke City	46	6	19	21	35	63	37

1990-91 SEASON

FIRST DIVISION

Arsenal	38	24	13	1	74	18	83
Liverpool	38	23	7	8	77	40	76
Crystal Palace	38	20	9	9	50	41	69
Leeds United	38	19	7	12	65	47	64
Manchester City	38	17	11	10	64	53	62
Manchester United	38	16	12	10	58	45	59
Wimbledon	38	14	14	10	53	46	56
Nottingham Forest	38	14	12	12	65	50	54
Everton	38	13	12	13	50	46	51
Tottenham	38	11	16	11	51	50	49
Chelsea	38	13	10	15	58	69	49
QPR	38	12	10	16	44	53	46
Sheffield United	38	13	7	18	36	55	46
Southampton	38	12	9	17	58	69	45
Norwich City	38	13	6	19	41	64	45
Coventry City	38	11	11	16	42	49	44
Aston Villa	38	9	14	15	46	58	41
Luton Town	38	10	7	21	42	61	37
Sunderland	**38**	**8**	**10**	**20**	**38**	**60**	**34**
Derby County	38	5	9	24	37	75	24

Arsenal 2 points deducted
Manchester United 1 point deducted

70

1991-92 SEASON

SECOND DIVISION

Team	P	W	D	L	F	A	Pts
Ipswich Town	46	24	12	10	70	50	84
Middlesbrough	46	23	11	12	58	41	80
Derby County	46	23	9	14	69	51	78
Leicester City	46	23	8	15	62	55	77
Cambridge United	46	19	17	10	65	47	74
Blackburn Rvrs	46	21	11	14	70	53	74
Charlton Athletic	46	20	11	15	54	48	71
Swindon Town	46	18	15	13	69	55	69
Portsmouth	46	19	12	15	65	51	69
Watford	46	18	11	17	51	48	65
Wolves	46	18	10	18	61	54	64
Southend United	46	17	11	18	63	63	62
Bristol Rovers	46	16	14	16	60	63	62
Tranmere Rovers	46	14	19	13	56	56	61
Millwall	46	17	10	19	64	71	61
Barnsley	46	16	11	19	46	57	59
Bristol City	46	13	15	18	55	71	54
Sunderland	**46**	**14**	**11**	**21**	**61**	**65**	**53**
Grimsby Town	46	14	11	21	47	62	53
Newcastle United	46	13	13	20	66	84	52
Oxford United	46	13	11	22	66	73	50
Plymouth Argyle	46	13	9	24	42	64	48
Brighton & Hove Alb.	46	12	11	23	56	77	47
Port Vale	46	10	15	21	42	59	45

1993-94 SEASON

FIRST DIVISION

Team	P	W	D	L	F	A	Pts
Crystal Palace	46	27	9	10	73	46	90
Nottingham Forest	46	23	14	9	74	49	83
Millwall	46	19	17	10	58	49	74
Leicester City	46	19	16	11	72	59	73
Tranmere Rovers	46	21	9	16	69	53	72
Derby County	46	20	11	15	73	68	71
Notts County	46	20	7	9	65	69	68
Wolves	46	17	17	12	60	47	68
Middlesbrough	46	18	13	15	66	54	67
Stoke City	46	18	13	15	57	59	67
Charlton Athletic	46	19	8	19	61	58	65
Sunderland	**46**	**19**	**8**	**19**	**54**	**57**	**65**
Bristol City	46	16	16	14	47	50	64
Bolton Wanderers	46	15	14	17	63	64	59
Southend United	46	17	8	21	63	67	59
Grimsby Town	46	13	20	13	52	47	59
Portsmouth	46	15	13	18	52	58	58
Barnsley	46	16	7	23	55	67	55
Watford	46	15	9	22	66	80	54
Luton Town	46	14	11	21	56	60	53
West Brom. Albion	46	13	12	21	60	69	51
Birmingham City	46	13	11	12	42	69	51
Oxford United	46	13	10	23	54	75	49
Peterborough United	46	8	13	25	48	76	37

1995-96 SEASON

FIRST DIVISION

Team	P	W	D	L	F	A	Pts
Sunderland	**46**	**22**	**17**	**7**	**59**	**33**	**83**
Derby County	46	21	16	8	69	48	79
Crystal Palace	46	20	15	11	67	48	75
Stoke City	46	20	13	13	60	49	73
Leicester City	46	19	14	13	66	60	71
Charlton Athletic	46	17	20	9	57	45	71
Ipswich Town	46	19	12	15	79	69	69
Huddersfield Town	46	17	12	17	61	58	63
Sheffield United	46	16	14	16	57	54	62
Barnsley	46	14	18	14	60	66	60
West Bromwich A.	46	16	12	18	60	68	60

1992-93 SEASON

FIRST DIVISION

Team	P	W	D	L	F	A	Pts
Newcastle United	46	29	9	8	92	38	96
West Ham United	46	26	10	10	81	41	88
Portsmouth	46	26	10	10	80	46	88
Tranmere Rovers	46	23	10	13	72	56	79
Swindon Town	46	21	13	12	74	59	76
Leicester City	46	22	10	14	71	64	76
Millwall	46	18	16	12	65	53	70
Derby County	46	19	9	18	68	57	66
Grimsby Town	46	19	7	20	58	57	64
Peterborough United	46	16	14	16	55	63	62
Wolves	46	16	13	17	57	56	61
Charlton Athletic	46	16	13	17	49	46	61
Barnsley	46	17	9	20	56	60	60
Oxford United	46	14	14	18	53	56	56
Bristol City	46	14	14	18	49	67	56
Watford	46	14	13	19	57	71	55
Notts County	46	12	16	18	55	70	52
Southend United	46	13	13	20	54	64	52
Birmingham City	46	13	12	21	50	72	51
Luton Town	46	10	21	15	48	62	51
Sunderland	**46**	**13**	**11**	**22**	**50**	**64**	**50**
Brentford	46	13	10	23	52	71	49
Cambridge United	46	11	16	19	48	69	49
Bristol Rovers	46	10	11	25	55	87	41

1994-95 SEASON

FIRST DIVISION

Team	P	W	D	L	F	A	Pts
Middlesbrough	46	23	13	10	67	40	82
Reading	46	23	10	13	58	44	79
Bolton Wanderers	46	21	14	11	67	45	76
Wolves	46	21	13	12	77	61	76
Tranmere Rovers	46	22	10	14	67	58	76
Barnsley	46	20	12	14	63	52	72
Watford	46	19	13	14	52	46	70
Sheffield United	46	17	17	12	74	55	68
Derby County	46	18	12	16	66	51	66
Grimsby Town	46	17	14	15	62	56	65
Stoke City	46	16	15	15	50	53	63
Millwall	46	16	14	16	60	60	62
Southend United	46	18	8	20	54	73	62
Oldham Athletic	46	16	13	17	60	60	61
Charlton Athletic	46	16	11	19	58	66	59
Luton Town	46	15	13	18	61	64	58
Port Vale	46	15	13	18	58	64	58
Portsmouth	46	15	13	18	53	63	58
West Brom. Albion	46	16	10	20	51	57	58
Sunderland	**46**	**12**	**18**	**16**	**41**	**45**	**54**
Swindon Town	46	12	12	22	54	73	48
Burnley	46	11	13	22	49	74	46
Bristol City	46	11	12	23	42	63	45
Notts County	46	9	13	24	45	66	40

Team	P	W	D	L	F	A	Pts
Port Vale	46	15	15	16	59	66	60
Tranmere Rovers	46	14	17	15	64	60	59
Southend United	46	15	14	17	52	61	59
Birmingham City	46	15	13	18	61	64	58
Norwich City	46	14	15	17	59	55	57
Grimsby Town	46	14	14	18	55	69	56
Oldham Athletic	46	14	14	18	54	50	56
Reading	46	13	17	16	54	63	56
Wolverhampton W	46	13	16	17	56	62	55
Portsmouth	46	13	13	20	61	69	52
Millwall	46	13	13	20	43	63	52
Watford	46	10	18	18	62	70	48
Luton Town	46	11	12	23	40	64	45